Secretariat

THOROUGHBRED Legends®

Secretariat

Racing's Greatest Triple Crown Winner

50TH ANNIVERSARY EDITION

TIMOTHY T. CAPPS

ECLIPSE PRESS

Essex, Connecticut

ECLIPSE PRESS

An imprint of Globe Pequot, the trade division of
The Rowman & Littlefield Publishing Group, Inc.
4501 Forbes Blvd., Ste. 200
Lanham, MD 20706
www.rowman.com

Distributed by NATIONAL BOOK NETWORK

British Library Cataloguing in Publication Information available

Library of Congress Control Number: 2002110115

ISBN 978-1-4930-7332-0 (paperback) | ISBN 978-1-4930-7895-0 (e-book)

♾™ The paper used in this publication meets the minimum requirements
of American National Standard for Information Sciences—Permanence of
Paper for Printed Library Materials, ANSI/NISO Z39.48-1992.

SECRETARIAT

CONTENTS

INTRODUCTION

A Dream Come True

W hen I was approached about writing this book, I was flattered and, simultaneously, apprehensive. Like many people, I was a huge fan of Secretariat, for reasons well beyond his "leading man" looks and stupendous performances.

His sire, Bold Ruler, was my first great love as a racehorse, and I watched in amazement and delight as he forged an almost unparalleled stud career. As the years passed though, his stallion record contained one glaring hole: no winners of a Triple Crown race, which led critics to conclude his progeny lacked the stamina required for classic company.

By the time Secretariat appeared as a two-year-old, I had largely given up hope that Bold Ruler, by then deceased, would ever sire a winner of a Triple Crown race or, for that matter, winners of those late summer and fall middle-distance events integral to winning year-end championships.

Secretariat, with his appearance and running style, immediately rekindled my forlorn hopes but also my fear that he was the last best hope, leaving no margin for error.

His subsequent career, of course, was a dream come true, although not without its valleys to offset those very high peaks. I found myself on emotional edge prior to his races and drained afterward; I was actually relieved when he retired from racing. Even though I had no connection with the horse, I felt as if a little part of him belonged to me.

My apprehension in writing this book was twofold: (1) how could I possibly convey my feelings and write a balanced, readable, factually accurate account of his life; (2) what could I add to the many words already written or spoken about him? Finally, I realized that if nothing new could be added to the Secretariat legend, there were always new ways of asking old questions or portraying forgotten images.

I was helped immeasurably by the immense number of words already penned about the horse, notably the two books that appeared within two years of his last race.

One, a coffee table book by Raymond G. "Raymie" Woolfe named *Secretariat*, was full of both photos from early foalhood through the end of his racing life and words written by a horseman who, his years of experience notwithstanding, had allowed himself to fall in love with the supremely handsome son of Bold Ruler.

The other was *Big Red of Meadow Stable*, a book with a hokey title and a ton of substance by longtime *Sports Illustrated* writer Bill Nack. This skilled reporter surpassed the call of duty in producing the most in-depth and insider look at the great racehorse. Nack did all the right things — researching thoroughly, asking pointed questions, providing behind-the-scenes details of the horse's day-to-day life and the personalities nearest to him — and then he added one more vital ingredient. Passion.

Nack felt a truly personal and deeply emotional attachment to his subject that let him define Secretariat's life — and death — in a way that told a gripping yet glorious tale, bringing into focus the hold Secretariat had on so many fans and industry professionals (the book was reprinted in 2002 as *Secretariat: The Making of a Champion*).

Nack, Woolfe, and the writings of Charlie Hatton, Kent Hollingsworth, Tony Morris, and Ed Bowen, among others, provided much fodder for this book. My own recollections began on a July day with a happenstance purchase at an Alexandria, Virginia, drugstore of a *Daily Racing Form* (the old broadsheet) that listed a chestnut colt by Bold Ruler out of Somethingroyal in its New York entries.

The dream, for me, began there and has never really ended. Secretariat appears in my mind's eye today as readily as he did in 1972 and '73: on his best day, the best racehorse I ever saw or expect to see. I even had my Secretariat race-watching outfit: blue-and-white checked shirt, dark blue slacks, mostly polyester, of course (this was the seventies, after all).

He was the fulfillment of my own modest hopes, an inspiration for a career in the most interesting and enriching of sporting endeavors, a place where, when all is said and done, we are only as good as our horses.

Secretariat was the Bold Ruler I had awaited, the horse American racing wanted and needed. I hope I have done him justice.

Timothy T. Capps
Columbia, Maryland 2002

SECRETARIAT

PROLOGUE

Long Live The Crown

The term "Triple Crown" was first used in horse racing in the mid-nineteenth century to describe England's then most-sought-after events for three-year-old Thoroughbreds: the Two Thousand Guineas at Newmarket, the Derby Stakes at Epsom Downs, and the St. Leger Stakes at Doncaster.

The races had been around awhile (the St. Leger was first run in 1776, the Derby in 1780, the Guineas in 1809) when, in 1853, West Australian finally swept the triumvirate. He was later to be acclaimed the first Triple Crown winner. Only fourteen others have followed thus far in England's storied racing history, most recently Nijinsky II in 1970.

The idea for an American Triple Crown patterned after the English version surfaced in New York in the latter part of the nineteenth century. The Withers

Stakes (one mile), the Belmont Stakes (one and a half miles), and the Lawrence Realization (then one and five-eighths miles) comprised the triple, with distances and scheduling very similar to their English counterparts, but the series never seemed to catch on with American horsemen.

By the early twentieth century, the Kentucky Derby, at Churchill Downs in Louisville; the Preakness Stakes, at Pimlico in Baltimore; and the Belmont Stakes, at Belmont Park in New York, had become individually important races. Their prizes, distances, and scheduling (all three were run in the spring) meant that most nice three-year-olds had one or more of these events on their schedules.

The three races were not connected, as is the case today, and the Derby and Preakness were often run only a few days apart, with the Preakness sometimes coming first. Therefore, it was not unusual for horses in the early part of the century to compete in both the Derby and Preakness, and, depending on their form, reappear in the Belmont, sometimes with a race or two (such as the Withers) in between.

The first horse to win the Derby, Preakness, and

Belmont was Sir Barton in 1919, and, like West Australian in 1853, he was not called a Triple Crown winner at the time.

In 1930, eleven years after Sir Barton's sweep, Gallant Fox captured the Derby, Preakness, and Belmont. At the time, the three races were starting to coalesce as a series. The day after Gallant Fox's Belmont victory, a story in the *New York Times*, written by Bryan Field (who would later manage Delaware Park), referred to Gallant Fox's Derby-Preakness-Belmont sweep as "the Triple Crown."

In the early thirties, *Daily Racing Form* columnist Charlie Hatton began referring to the threesome as the Triple Crown, with all the exuberant praise his pen could muster, and by the time Omaha and War Admiral had won the three races in 1935 and 1937, respectively, the term was routinely used by writers and radio broadcasters nationwide.

Thus, the view that the media concocted the Triple Crown with the sheer magnitude of its coverage, especially of the Derby, may have been merited. However, without substance the hype wouldn't have lasted.

The Triple Crown was competitive and grueling; it

demanded all the talent and tenacity a Thoroughbred could exhibit. It took a good horse to win one of the three races, an exceptional one to win two, and something extraordinary to sweep the series.

That it was done four times from 1941 through 1948 (Whirlaway, 1941; Count Fleet, 1943; Assault, 1946; Citation, 1948) is remarkable and a testimonial to the class and durability of the horses that accomplished the feat, especially in light of what was to follow.

Citation waged a remarkable three-year-old campaign in 1948. He won nineteen of twenty starts, including the Triple Crown races, and in many circles, was thought to be the equal of Man o' War.

After Citation, even if there were no foreseeable star on the horizon, history suggested a Triple Crown winner would be along shortly. With seven Triple Crown winners in the last two decades, the feat seemed easily attainable.

By the early 1950s, the series was clearly the place to be for a three-year-old male in the spring. But with the growing visibility of the Triple Crown resulting in pointing horses toward the series, winning any or all of the three races was becoming more difficult.

Still, it was hard to imagine many years going by without a Triple Crown winner, a new celebrity horse for fans to admire and a nation to follow on the fast-growing medium of network television.

The great gray of the early fifties, Native Dancer, barely lost the Triple Crown when he was beaten by a head in the 1953 Derby before winning the Preakness and Belmont and becoming racing's first television star.

Over the next few decades, there would be several standout Thoroughbreds who would win two Triple Crown races — Nashua, Tim Tam, Carry Back, Northern Dancer, Damascus, and Majestic Prince, among others — but no new Triple Crown winner.

By now, with more than two decades having passed since Citation's Triple Crown sweep, racing journalists and many industry participants were beginning to question whether the Triple Crown was winnable anymore.

Were the races too close together? Should they be shortened — at least the Derby and Belmont? Were Thoroughbreds now too frail to handle the rigors of three top-level competitions in five weeks?

Purists snorted and said, "What was good enough

for Gallant Fox, Count Fleet, or Citation should be good enough for succeeding generations. The Triple Crown should be tough to win; besides, these races probably get too much hype anyway, when the focus should be on other key races, especially in the fall. The racing season is all year, not simply five weeks in the spring."

Regardless of the merits of the various arguments, by the early seventies two post-World War II trends in American racing had evolved in ways that made the Triple Crown less attainable than in its early years.

One was the significant increase in winter racing, which provided earlier and more varied options for the trainers of Triple Crown prospects and presented new preparation challenges.

The second, and perhaps more important, was the dramatic increase in the foal crops.

Sir Barton's crop, foals of 1916, numbered 2,128; Gallant Fox's crop was 4,182; Omaha's, 5,256; War Admiral's, 4,924; Whirlaway's, 5,696; Count Fleet's, 6,003; Assault's, 5,923; Citation's, 5,819.

The North American foal crop topped ten thousand for the first time in 1956, reached twenty thousand in

1966, and was at 24,361 by 1970. Racing had grown to accommodate the increase, but there could be little doubt that in the late sixties and onward, a Triple Crown aspirant faced tougher odds than did his predecessors. Bigger foal crops meant more competition at all levels.

As the sport headed into the seventies, the question of whether another Triple Crown winner would emerge weighed heavily, especially in light of other changes affecting American racing. Fan attendance, if adjusted for the additional racing days being added to track schedules throughout the country, was stagnant, at best. Although growing, wagering handle, like attendance, was going sideways or downward if adjusted for both additional racing days and inflation.

Shrewd observers of racing also noted something else in the early seventies: the sport was losing the battle on the network television front. Being on television had proven to be a boon to many sports, especially professional football and golf, while network television generally confined its exposure of racing to the Triple Crown and perhaps a few preps for those events.

Racing supposedly was not a good television sport

because it lacked continuous action and, truth be told, many racing executives were not keen on televising races. They believed it would severely damage gate receipts and did not visualize television's marketing opportunities.

A Triple Crown winner would certainly excite mass media interest, especially television coverage, but could it realistically happen? Was the American Triple Crown an anachronism because it had remained unwinnable for so long? As configured, was it even winnable? Was horse racing's most meaningful event in danger of becoming irrelevant to anyone outside of racing's inner circles?

CHAPTER 1

Son Of Thunder

Doswell, Virginia, is another of those sleepy towns along U.S. Route 1 that once were the bane of truckers and tourists, who stopped and started their way along the nation's major North-South thoroughfare in the days before vast interstate highways.

Doswell is now familiar, if at all, as the Interstate 95 exit for Paramount's Kings Dominion, a popular amusement park. Drivers speeding toward Washington, D.C., or Richmond, Virginia, may have noticed the exit sign.

A few miles away from I-95 and its array of gas stations, chain hotels, and restaurants, towns like Doswell and those throughout the rest of Caroline and Hanover counties aren't much different than they were decades ago, sleepy rural towns that are now largely bedroom communities for Richmond.

The central Virginia area they occupy is the western edge of the Tidewater section of the state, and, like much of the surrounding area, has a significant historical heritage. Hanover County is the birthplace of the famed orator and politician Patrick Henry, who is best known for a fiery pre-American Revolution public speech, with which he concluded, "As for me, give me liberty or give me death." His life inspired twentieth century historian Henry Mayer to title his biography of Henry, *A Son of Thunder*, a term that uniquely describes the flamboyant Henry, who was noted for his powerful oratory and staunch defense of individual liberties. He was a larger-than-life and sometimes controversial character, and an important factor in the evolution of the Bill of Rights in the U.S. Constitution.

Hanover County also is the death site of cavalry commander and Civil War legend General James Ewell Brown "Jeb" Stuart. The "eyes and ears" of Robert E. Lee, Stuart died in 1864 after being wounded at Yellow Tavern as the Confederate star continued to wane. Revolutionary War hero George Rogers Clark and William Clark (the Clark in the Lewis and Clark expedition) grew up in neighboring Caroline County, where

Stonewall Jackson and John Wilkes Booth drew their last breaths.

Topographically, the region is made up mostly of gently rolling lowlands punctuated by rivers, streams, and swamps. In the summer the steamy air sticks to the skin. Mosquitoes and other hot-weather bugs abound. Heavy rains can quickly push waterways like the North Anna River and its companion, the South Anna, over their banks and into surrounding lowlands.

The two Annas, in fact, proved inhospitable enough that Union General Ulysses S. Grant decided not to confront Lee's troops along their banks. Instead, he circled the area and moved south of Richmond to Petersburg for what would be the climactic campaign of the Civil War in the East.

More than five decades before Virginia became the Civil War's premier battleground, Charles Dabney Morris established The Meadow, a large family farm on the banks of the North Anna River near Doswell. The family would lose the farm in the traumatic Reconstruction era, but a family member, Christopher Chenery, would buy it back in 1936.

Chenery was a Richmond native who grew up in

Ashland, Virginia, a few miles south of Doswell and The Meadow. He studied engineering at Washington and Lee College, eventually getting into the public utility business by consolidating several private water and gas companies and taking them public.

Chenery, who was always interested in horses, had the resources by 1936 to begin converting his enthusiasm into a serious pastime. He drained swampland and developed The Meadow's 2,600 acres into a working horse farm, then began buying fillies and mares for a broodmare band.

Three years later Chenery made the first of two purchases that would dramatically impact his racing and breeding world while establishing a perpetual legacy for The Meadow.

The first, out of the Edward F. Simms dispersal sale, was a yearling filly named Hildene for whom Chenery paid $750. Although well-bred enough, she appeared expensive even at $750 after failing to win in eight starts and earning one hundred dollars. Nonetheless, Chenery kept her for breeding, and in that arena she became a superstar.

Hildene's second foal, Mangohick (by Sun Beau),

was a minor stakes winner, but her fourth foal, Hill Prince, won the 1950 Preakness, was Horse of the Year that season, and was champion of his division at ages two, three, and four. Hill Prince's younger full brothers, Prince Hill and Third Brother, were both capable handicappers in the mid-1950s. All were sons of Princequillo, an ex-claimer who became a quality distance horse.

Princequillo started his stud career for the Hancock family of Claiborne Farm fame at their Virginia farm, Ellerslie Stud, for a $250 fee and literally made himself a leading sire. He was eventually moved to Claiborne in Kentucky, where he became arguably the best broodmare sire in U.S. history, a matter of considerable importance to this story.

Hildene's next-to-last offspring, the Turn-to colt First Landing, was champion two-year-old male in 1958, earned almost $800,000 in a three-year-career, and was a decent stallion, getting Riva Ridge, the dual classic winner in 1972 for Meadow Stable, the name in which Chenery's horses raced.

The second of Chenery's life-changing purchases was Imperatrice. Like Hildene, she was a foal of 1938 but a runner of much higher quality and, therefore, much more expensive.

Bred by William H. LaBoyteaux, Imperatrice was a filly with a reasonable pedigree whose racing and production exploits greatly enhanced her pedigree page. She was by Caruso, an early maturing son of Polymelian (broodmare sire of Polynesian, and a son of the great stallion Polymelus, sire of the seminal sire Phalaris). Caruso had speed and some durability but would soon fade into obscurity as a stallion, Imperatrice being his only important offspring.

Imperatrice's female family didn't have a lot to recommend it until one got back to the third dam, Cinq a Sept, who won the 1927 Irish Oaks and several stakes in England for American department store pioneer Marshall Field.

On the track, though, Imperatrice outran her pedigree. Trained by a former leading jockey, George Odom, she started thirty-one times in her three-year career, winning eleven races, among them four stakes, including Saratoga's Test Stakes and the Fall Highweight Handicap, beating males, as a four-year-old. Although possessed of good acceleration, she could carry her speed through middle distances, and her quality assured that she would be sent to representative stallions at the outset of her broodmare career.

Her first foal, the filly Imperieuse, didn't win but did produce a stakes winner. Imperatrice's second foal was the Whirlaway filly Scattered, who won the Coaching Club American Oaks and Pimlico Oaks in 1948 and became a successful broodmare.

Imperatrice's next two foals, Imperium and Squared Away, were by a LaBoyteaux-owned "house" sire, Piping Rock. While both offspring were stakes-winning sprinters, Squared Away became one of the best speed horses of his generation, winning eight stakes and placing in fourteen others.

By the time those two were displaying their racing merit, LaBoyteaux had died and Chenery had paid $30,000 for Imperatrice at a dispersal sale. The purchase did not pay immediate dividends. Imperatrice's first three foals for him won seven races and just over $30,000, collectively, although one, Queens Moon, would become a good producer.

Imperatrice's fourth foal for The Meadow was by Princequillo, who had elevated the blue-and-white block silks of Meadow Stable to prominence in 1949 and 1950 through his son Hill Prince. The foal's name was, appropriately as future circumstances would have it, Somethingroyal, and she was born in 1952.

Somethingroyal would have to live up to her name in the breeding shed, for her racing career consisted of a single maiden race at Saratoga in 1954 in which she finished sixth. Bred the following year to home sire Bryan G., she produced an unraced gelding named Havidar, then foaled the stakes-placed filly Cherryville, by Correspondent.

Imperatrice, in the meantime, went on to produce three more stakes winners, including the good filly Speedwell, from the first crop of the brilliant racehorse, Bold Ruler.

In 1958 Somethingroyal was bred to the highly regarded young sire Turn-to, whose career was ended prematurely by a bowed tendon he suffered as the favorite before the 1954 Kentucky Derby. The resultant foal, to be named Sir Gaylord, arrived in the spring of 1959, following the sensational 1958 campaign of Meadow Stable's First Landing, a member of Turn-to's first crop.

Sir Gaylord's pedigree suggested a middle-distance performer in the making, but he demonstrated uncommon quickness by the summer of his juvenile season, winning four stakes races in succession, among them Monmouth Park's Sapling Stakes. The Sapling win made him the erstwhile leader of his division, but consecutive third-place finishes in the Hopeful, Futurity, Cowdin, and Champagne stakes left him adrift of the unbeaten Ridan, among others, in year-end championship voting. Some viewed him as a bit of a disappointment, perhaps a fast-maturing sprinter, although his pedigree indicated otherwise.

The following winter, though, Sir Gaylord was the rage of American racing, beating Ridan in the Bahamas Stakes at Hialeah, then winning the Everglades Stakes at the same track in a style that made him the early Kentucky Derby favorite. He missed the Flamingo with a minor injury and then won an allowance race to set him up for the Derby.

On the Friday before the classic, Sir Gaylord returned from a morning gallop somewhat worse for the experience, displaying a slight limp. That lameness turned out to be the result of a hairline fracture of a sesamoid bone, which led to his retirement from racing, potential unrealized.

Retired to stud at Claiborne Farm, Sir Gaylord became one of the best sires of the sixties and seventies and was as responsible as any other horse for the American invasion of European racing that would truly internationalize the Thoroughbred sport. Among his sixty stakes winners were champions Sir Ivor and Habitat, the former a splendid colt who won numerous high-class races in Europe, including the 1968 English Derby, then finished his career with a stylish victory in the Washington, D.C., International at Laurel.

Sir Ivor had it all — looks, conformation, speed, toughness, and versatility — and he would become a successful sire, especially of fillies.

Habitat was the best miler in Europe in 1969 and an immediate hit at stud, cranking out top-notch sprinters and milers in production-line fashion.

By the time Sir Gaylord was at his racing peak, Somethingroyal had two additional foals nibbling at The Meadow's grass, one a colt by Double Jay named Mostar who would become stakes-placed, the other a son of home sire First Landing named First Family. He would go on to win four stakes, including the 1966 Gulfstream Park Handicap, and was second or third in several others, among them a third-place finish in the 1965 Belmont Stakes.

In 1964 Somethingroyal produced a stakes-placed full sister to First Family named Grand Coulee, then was mated, for the first time, to the emerging super sire, Bold Ruler. The result of that match was a filly named Syrian Sea, who won the Selima, Colleen, and Astarita stakes at age two in 1967 and was stakes-placed in good company in 1968.

By the time Syrian Sea made her mark at the race-track, The Meadow operation was facing, after more than forty years of success, a transitional challenge. Chris Chenery's health was failing, and by the fall of 1967 his three children had begun to intervene in the farm and racing stable's affairs.

Two of them, Dr. Hollis Chenery, then chief econo-mist for the World Bank, and Margaret Carmichael, who lived in Tucson, Arizona, and ran her own busi-ness, had neither the time nor inclination to immerse themselves in The Meadow.

The third sibling, Helen "Penny" Chenery Tweedy,

was the only logical and likely candidate to pick up her father's mantle. She was a horse lover at an early age, riding regularly in shows or for pleasure. She served with the American Red Cross in Europe during World War II and then returned to New York to seek a master's degree in business at Columbia University. She married Jack Tweedy, whom she had met in New York while in graduate school, and was involved in The Meadow operation as a corporate board member, but was really more of an observer until her father's illness necessitated a larger role.

She started reading industry trade journals faithfully and seeking advice from both Meadow employees and her father's friends and colleagues, particularly A.B. "Bull" Hancock Jr., perhaps the ultimate Kentucky "hardboot."

Bull Hancock, whose father A.B. Hancock helped Chris Chenery get into the Thoroughbred business, had taken over Claiborne at a time when his own father's health was declining. The younger Hancock was widely credited with saving Claiborne, then building it into the world's pre-eminent stallion operation. Bull Hancock was smart, decisive, and skilled at dealing with Claiborne's myriad of clients, which included many of the who's who of American racing, especially the "captains of industry" sorts — like Chris Chenery — who were mostly private breeders.

Hancock had a reputation for being a straight shooter, which is what Chris Chenery's youngest child, Penny Chenery, needed.

The Meadow had, due to the vision and adventuresome spirit of Chris Chenery, grown into a substantial breeding and racing operation and was in need of some careful pruning. Unfortunately, Chenery no longer had the capacity to make the critical decisions that would determine the future viability of his racing empire.

Following the death of their mother in November 1967, the Chenery children met and determined that Penny would take over The Meadow.

She became a regular at the racetrack and conversed frequently with Elizabeth Ham, her father's longtime executive secretary and The Meadow's financial manager, and Howard Gentry, the farm manager, as well as with Bull Hancock and her own new hire, young trainer Roger Laurin.

The son of successful veteran trainer Lucien Laurin,

Roger had a budding reputation as a thoughtful, patient, knowledgeable horseman. He would help Penny Tweedy through the uncertainties of selling surplus horses and keeping the racing stable's expenses under control.

Perhaps Chris Chenery's most valuable equine legacy was the quality broodmare band that roamed The Meadow's ample paddocks.

By the late sixties, Hildene was deceased and Imperatrice pensioned, but Somethingroyal and other relatives of the two foundation mares were still around and very productive. One was the stakes-producing mare Hasty Matelda, who was coupled with Somethingroyal in what would be a history-making venture.

Bold Ruler had been retired in 1958 to take up stud duties the following year at Claiborne. He had raced under the ownership of Gladys Phipps' Wheatley Stable and would continue to be controlled by the Phipps family as a stallion, rather than be syndicated, as was becoming the custom of the day with leading racehorses whose pedigrees made them attractive sire prospects.

Thus, Bold Ruler would be bred to the Phipps mares and to outside mares as they saw fit, meaning he would mostly consort with Claiborne client mares and not many of his offspring would find their way to the auction ring.

Conventional wisdom today says a stallion's best chance for success comes when leading trainers have access to his progeny, particularly at auctions, giving him wide exposure. While the commercial breeding industry was not as significant as it would become by the late seventies, Bold Ruler's relative absence from it had absolutely no impact on his success or popularity. His first crop to race, foals of 1960 (including Meadow Stable's Speedwell, Bold Ruler's first stakes winner), did so well that he was soon the most sought-after stallion in the country.

In what would be a precursor of today's foal-sharing arrangements, the Phippses and Bull Hancock agreed to forgo a stud fee for Bold Ruler in exchange for getting to keep one of two foals produced by the mare he bred in successive seasons or two mares he bred in the same season. Whether the Phippses or the mare owner got first choice came down to the flip of a coin before the foal was born.

This gave the Phippses an opportunity to get the best mares to Bold Ruler and, when the toss went their way, add well-bred fillies to their own formidable broodmare band. The arrangement also gave the mare owners a chance to get to the most glamorous sire in America.

Chris Chenery wanted to send his mares, Hasty Matelda and Somethingroyal, to Bold Ruler in 1968 and agreed to the coin-toss arrangement with Ogden Phipps, son of Gladys Phipps and head of the Phipps family's racing and breeding interests. Both mares were bred to Bold Ruler in 1968, with Somethingroyal foaling a filly and Hasty Matelda a colt in the spring of 1969.

Bred back to Bold Ruler, Somethingroyal got pregnant, but Cicada, the champion Meadow Stable race mare who replaced Hasty Matelda in the successive round of breeding, was barren. This made the coin toss scheduled for later that year an interesting proposition.

By the terms of the agreement, the winner of the toss could pick the foal he wanted, but could only take one. The loser would get the other two, assuming Somethingroyal delivered successfully in 1970.

Penny Tweedy, who had already decided to decline

further participation in the coin-toss deals, was ambivalent about the result, perhaps preferring to lose and get the "two-fer."

In the fall of 1969, the principals gathered in the office of New York Racing Association chairman Alfred Vanderbilt for the coin flip, accompanied by Bull Hancock, adviser to both the Phippses and Chenerys.

Vanderbilt flipped the coin, Ogden Phipps called "tails," and the fifty-cent piece landed with tails showing.

The Phippses went the safe route and took the weanling filly out of Somethingroyal, whom they named The Bride. The Meadow was left with the weanling colt out of Hasty Matelda, who would be named Rising River, and the unborn Somethingroyal foal.

As a historic footnote, let it be noted that neither The Bride nor Rising River accomplished anything of value on the racetrack, The Bride because she was too slow, Rising River because he was too unsound. The Bride couldn't run, but she produced two stakes winners and is the granddam of two others, demonstrating once again that good genes matter, even if it takes a while for them to emerge.

The yet-to-appear Somethingroyal baby? Perhaps another "Son of Thunder" coming out of central Virginia, another flamboyant, larger-than-life character who would capture public imagination and achieve a prominent place in history? One could only hope.

CHAPTER 2

Royal Rulers

Perhaps it was a harbinger of things to come that Somethingroyal, a nonentity as a racehorse, was the product of parents who were overachievers on the racetrack and at stud, horses who earned their acclaim through steady excellence rather than fashionable pedigrees or early brilliance.

Somethingroyal's sire, the previously mentioned Princequillo, was an Irish-bred. If World War II had not broken out, Princequillo would have remained in Europe to race and later to breed, had he proven worthy of a stud opportunity.

Princequillo was by Prince Rose, declared the best horse ever to race in Belgium, for what that's worth, though he likely was a good-class Thoroughbred. Princequillo was out of the good French filly Cosquilla, herself by English Derby winner Papyrus. There was stamina throughout this pedigree along with late maturity, not the sort of stuff to excite the typical American breeder, even if accompanied by a high degree of class.

Foaled in 1940, Princequillo was shipped to the United States that fall and arrived as a rather small, unprepossessing weanling with a pedigree that might as well have been from Mars. He started off in the lowest ranks of racing as a two-year-old and stayed there for much of his juvenile year, eventually being claimed by trainer Horatio Luro, who grabbed him for one of his owners, in part because he was angry with the colt's breeder and owner, L.L. Lawrence. Luro felt Lawrence had treated him with indifference in a would-be horse deal.

Even Luro's skills couldn't elevate Princequillo above the moderate ($2,500–$3,500) claiming level, at least at sprint distances. The following year (1943), however, Luro shifted him to longer races, and the results were revealing, even in better company. Princequillo won the Saratoga Handicap (one and a quarter miles), the Saratoga Cup (one and three-quarters miles), and the Jockey Club Gold Cup (two miles), beating some of the best horses in training. He generally carried less weight than his contemporaries but, nonetheless, proved he belonged.

Princequillo's four-year-old season, during which Dave Englander trained him, was not as successful, although the colt won the Questionnaire Handicap (one and five-eighths miles) at Jamaica and the Merchants' and Citizens' Handicap (one and three-sixteenths miles) at Belmont. He demonstrated in those, and other races, that he was not quite up to beating the best at middle distances without meaningful weight concessions, but that he could hold his own as the distances lengthened.

An injury at age four necessitated his retirement. This event was of no great consequence to anyone but Bull Hancock who, after watching him win the Saratoga Cup at three, wanted him as a stallion prospect. Claiborne bought a quarter interest in him and sent him to Ellerslie Stud, the Hancocks' ancestral home near Charlottesville, Virginia.

His $250 stud fee notwithstanding, this staying son of a horse unfamiliar to American breeders had difficulty attracting mares. Fortunately, several of the ones he got came from Claiborne clients like Chris Chenery and William Woodward, and from Claiborne itself.

From those early matings Princequillo sired horses

such as Hill Prince and Woodward's English standout Prince Simon, a narrow loser of the 1947 English Two Thousand Guineas and Derby, giving the young stallion an opportunity to move to Kentucky, breed more and better mares, and command higher stud fees.

He would, before his death in 1964, become a remarkable success story, leading the North American sire list in 1957 and 1958 and siring sixty-five stakes winners (13.5 percent of his registered and named foals, a superior percentage).

His best performer was 1958 Horse of the Year Round Table, who became America's first great turf specialist and retired as the world's leading money earner. Round Table, like Prince John and other sons of Princequillo, became a superior stallion but will be best remembered as the standard by which good grass horses are measured in this country.

The Princequillos typically liked middle and longer distances and were durable and versatile. They were often at their best in the classics and the major handicaps that best define American racing. One is left to wonder how they would have fared had European buyers been prowling American yearling auctions in the 1950s as they did from the seventies onward.

Princequillo was amazingly successful as a brood-mare sire, leading the North American list eight times and having numerous champions among his grandsons and granddaughters. His success as a broodmare sire is interesting on a couple of levels. The prototypical broodmare sire is thought to come from a high-quality female family and to be a particularly good sire of racing fillies that, in turn, are bred to top sires, enhancing their chances of siring good racehorses.

Princequillo was an outstanding filly sire, but his female family was undistinguished. He certainly benefited from the Claiborne connection to leading breeders and their outstanding bloodstock, which assured him of good patronage and allowed him to produce daughters, who, in turn, became good broodmares. The Claiborne relationship is certainly one of the reasons for the so-called "nick" between the great English-bred sire Nasrullah and his sons, which included Nashua and Bold Ruler, and the daughters of Princequillo.

While the theory of nicks is often debated in racing circles, most breeders believe, possibly because it is fun and convenient to do so, that certain bloodlines have a particular affinity for others. Empirical evidence for such affinities is sometimes sketchy, but if breeders believe in them, then there must be something to the idea.

Most people who study such matters think that, while the fact that both stallions stood at Claiborne had something to do with the Nasrullah-Princequillo nick, there really was an unusual affinity between the two lines. Princequillo sired horses of stamina, durability, and even temperament while the Nasrullahs often had exceptional speed, soundness issues, and attitude problems. The blend, when it worked, could produce a special racehorse.

If Princequillo was the soul of middle-class stability, Bold Ruler was a high-society playboy who had the quintessential Euro-American pedigree, with intriguing blends of speed, stamina, precocity, and late maturity.

Bold Ruler's dam, Miss Disco, was a tough old gal who started fifty-four times in five years and recorded her stakes wins in sprints. The next two dams, Outdone and Sweep Out, were similar in merit and in type, being durable and, at the same time, speed oriented. Miss Disco's sire, Discovery, was a star over middle and classic routes. He was one of the truly great weight carriers in American racing annals, repeatedly hauling 130 or more pounds to victory. The bottom half of Bold Ruler's pedigree was, then, typically American-made, with speed, stoutness, and toughness in about equal amounts.

The top half of Bold Ruler's pedigree was, alternatively, full of flash and class. His sire, Nasrullah, was by the unbeaten Nearco, certainly one of Thoroughbred history's most influential stallions, out of a mare whose own dam, Mumtaz Mahal, a dazzling sprinter, was regarded as possibly the fastest filly ever seen in England. This was the famed speed family of Americus Girl, who would produce so many high-class runners and stud successes, such as Fair Trial, Abernant, and Tudor Minstrel.

On paper Nasrullah, bred and raced by the Aga Khan, had a right to be anything. On the racecourse he proved to be something else. He was beautifully conformed, with good size and balance and a wonderful way of moving, one of those rare specimens that make fillies sigh and other colts snort with envy. He also was one of racing's great head cases, his temperament being described by terms such as difficult (charitable) and mulish (accurate). In the United States, he probably would have been gelded despite the richness of his pedigree.

In fact, his often unseemly racecourse behavior made it difficult to assess his true merits as a racehorse. He won five of his ten career starts, among them the Champion Stakes at Newmarket, and was third in the 1943 English Derby, but he was obstinate enough in almost all his outings to suggest that there was always more in the tank.

He did not appear to be a true distance or cup horse, and given the speed influences in his pedigree, it is probable that he was at his best (when so inclined) over nine to ten furlongs. In other words, he was an early prototype of today's international classic horse.

As a sire Nasrullah was a phenomenon. He led the English sire list in 1951, the year after he came to America, and then led the North American list five times. He sired ninety-eight stakes winners, twenty-three percent of his 420 named foals. Had his stud career occurred during the era of big stallion books, he likely would have sired well over two hundred stakes winners and left behind virtually unmatchable records.

He sired classic winners in both Europe and America, sprinters and stayers, top colts and world-class fillies. Many of his sons became good stallions, and his daughters were prized as broodmares. He was, simply put, the best stallion in the world in his heyday, especially as a sire of racehorses, which is what stallions are supposed to do.

It is hard to choose the best from among his many good sons, but for most observers it comes down to Nashua or Bold Ruler. Nashua was sounder and appeared to have more stamina, winning both the Preakness and Belmont and two runnings of the two-mile Jockey Club Gold Cup. Bold Ruler seemed more resolute and carried high weights more frequently and successfully than Nashua; Nashua was splendidly con-formed, like his sire a picture of what a Thoroughbred should be. Bold Ruler, while well proportioned, was more angular and lighter than Nashua, but possessed of well-angled shoulders and picture-book hind legs. He looked racier than Nashua, if not as sturdy.

Bold Ruler was foaled at Claiborne Farm on April 6,

1954, oddly enough on the same day and at the same place as his great rival, Round Table, both destined to be great runners and great sires, although very different in looks and racing style.

From the outset Bold Ruler was an accident waiting to happen. He had a baseball-sized hernia as a foal and almost cut his tongue into two pieces in a training accident as a yearling that left him unhappy with anything that manipulated his mouth, such as a bit.

He showed legendary trainer "Sunny Jim" Fitzsimmons great speed from the beginning and broke his maiden quickly in April 1956 after the stable had moved from Florida to New York. After going unbeaten in five starts, Bold Ruler wrenched some back muscles and missed a few weeks of training. He came back to win the Futurity Stakes before he clipped heels in the Garden State Stakes and lost his momentum.

The Garden State Stakes and his terrible trip in the Remsen Stakes that followed cost him a shot at the two-year-old championship, but he was still well regarded by Fitzsimmons and jockey Eddie Arcaro, the team that had piloted Nashua to Horse of the Year honors the year before. Bold Ruler clearly had talent, despite his penchant for hurting himself and his "gotta be in front from start to finish" style that might have been related to his sensitive mouth, which made him resist restraint.

At three Bold Ruler had a year that began well and ended better, with lots of ups and downs in between.

He opened by equaling the track record for seven furlongs in the Bahamas Stakes at Hialeah and then lost to Calumet's brilliant Gen. Duke by a head in the Everglades, beat Gen. Duke in the Flamingo, setting a track record for a mile and one-eighth in 1:47, and then lost to him in world-record-equaling time (1:46 4/5) in the Florida Derby.

An injury forced Gen. Duke from the scene, but new competition appeared in the form of Irish import Gallant Man, who ran Bold Ruler to a nose in the Wood Memorial, with the latter setting a track record of 1:48 4/5 for a mile and one-eighth.

Bold Ruler could only finish fourth as the favorite in the Kentucky Derby, but Arcaro blamed himself for trying to restrain the colt too much in the early going.

In the Preakness, Bold Ruler had gauze and cotton over his sensitive tongue, and he was on the lead throughout, although pressured, winning comfortably enough over Derby winner Iron Liege.

At Belmont Park, Gallant Man was back on the scene with a new friend, a stablemate named Bold Nero, who was entered in the Belmont to try to get Bold Ruler to run faster than he should in the early stages of the race.

The tactic worked to perfection; Bold Ruler ran the first quarter in :23 2/5, the second in :23 2/5, and was still in front, if leg weary, after a mile and a quarter in 2:01 2/5. After that, it was the Gallant Man show, and the little colt drew away to win in 2:26 3/5, a new American record for a mile and a half, with Bold Ruler twelve lengths away in third.

Fitzsimmons was as canny as they come, but he was also old school in his horse management thinking. He took care of his horses, but he didn't coddle them.

Still, Sunny Jim knew when to hold 'em and when to fold 'em, and after the 1957 Belmont, he gave the tired Bold Ruler a break. Always arthritic, the colt had a series of minor setbacks, including a bad reaction to a vaccination, a splint on his left foreleg, and a sore shoulder.

When he reappeared on September 9 at Belmont, the verve was back. He won a six-furlong allowance race in 1:10 1/5, while hauling 128 pounds and then took the Jerome Handicap by six lengths under 130 pounds, beating a nice field and running the mile in 1:35 on a sloppy track.

His next start was in the prestigious Woodward Stakes, a weight-for-age race over a mile and a quarter and the top middle-distance event of the fall. There he faced Gallant Man and leading older horse Dedicate, a son of Princequillo. Bold Ruler took the lead on the final turn but was passed by both the winning Dedicate and Gallant Man.

At that point his chances at Horse of the Year or champion three-year-old male honors seemed scant, and Fitzsimmons dropped Bold Ruler back to sprinting in the Vosburgh Handicap. Carrying 130 pounds, the three-year-old won by nine lengths over older horses and set a track record of 1:21 2/5 for seven furlongs, breaking a fifty-one-year-old record.

He then hauled 133 pounds to an easy win in the mile and one-sixteenth Queens County Handicap and took up 136 pounds while winning over the same distance in the Benjamin Franklin Handicap at Garden State.

The latter race was intended to be his prep for Garden State's Trenton Handicap, which was run a week after the Franklin. (Can you imagine a trainer today running a horse under a 136 pounds a week before, say, the Breeders' Cup Classic?)

The Trenton turned out to be a match race among Bold Ruler, Gallant Man, and Round Table, the latter having spent the summer making a large name for himself, mostly in the Midwest. Dedicate was also on the tab but was withdrawn due to illness.

This, then, was the summit meeting for 1957, and Bold Ruler, the only speed horse in the race, took full advantage of his tactical edge, taking the early lead, widening it into the homestretch, then easily holding off Gallant Man in a good 2:01 3/5 for a mile and a quarter. This was Bold Ruler's first win at ten furlongs, and he could not have picked a better spot.

Fitzsimmons decided to call it a year for his colt, who would be named Horse of the Year and champion three-year-old male. Perhaps the highest compliment paid to him, though, came from New York racing secretary and handicapper Frank E. "Jimmy" Kilroe, who assigned him the incredibly high weight of 139 pounds for both the Knickerbocker and Roamer handicaps.

Remarkably, Bold Ruler had carried 130 pounds or more to victory four times in the fall and had won eleven of sixteen starts, his fourth place in the Kentucky Derby being his worst finish.

The three-year-olds of 1957 were a stellar group, one of the best crops ever to race in this country. To head that class was a memorable accomplishment.

At four Bold Ruler was quite likely better than at three, although his campaign was much shorter and a variety of leg ailments continued to bother him. A winter ankle injury delayed his season debut until May, when he appeared in the six-furlong Toboggan Handicap, in which he carried 133 pounds to victory over a talented field that included Clem, Cohoes, and Tick Tock, coming home in 1:09.

Afterward, he raced six more times before an injury in the Brooklyn Handicap forced his retirement. He carried at least 133 pounds in each race and won four of the six, including the ten-furlong Suburban and Monmouth handicaps under 134 pounds. His losses were to Gallant Man in the Metropolitan Handicap (carrying 135 pounds to the winner's 130) and to injury in the Brooklyn.

Although there would be no Horse of the Year award for him, he was named champion sprinter in North America and might have been, at level weights, the best anything in the country, Gallant Man and Round Table notwithstanding.

He went back to Claiborne with twenty-three wins in thirty-three starts, $764,204 in earnings, a lot of hardware, and a reputation as a sterling weight carrier. Altogether, he faced the starter eleven times with 130 pounds or more on his back and came back to the winner's circle at the end of nine of those races.

He had overcome chronic physical ailments and stiff competition to compile an enviable record, and with a good pedigree and good connections, he had excellent stud prospects.

To say he made the most of them would be to shortchange what became an epic stud career. He was the forerunner of what has become the most sought after modern stallion prospect: the high-class miler or middle-distance performer with matching pedigree.

His superior class, talent, and competitiveness muted any misgivings over his soundness or distance capacity, and Claiborne had no trouble getting him mares. Breeders who signed on early were quickly rewarded, for his first crop came out running and things only improved with subsequent groups.

The Bold Rulers were typically precocious, had the ability to compete in top company, and retained the class to keep doing so. His first foals arrived in 1960 and were led on the racetrack by the champion filly Lamb Chop, who won the ten-furlong Coaching Club American Oaks, among other major stakes. By the time his second crop arrived at the races in 1963, Bold Ruler, with no progeny older than three, led the North American sire list and the juvenile sire list.

Nor was he an early flash whose sizzle fizzled; the quality, and quantity, kept coming, enough that Bold Ruler would lead the general sire list by progeny earnings seven consecutive years, a modern record for North America.

Bold Ruler also led the juvenile sire list six times, and most of his stakes winners (he averaged almost 6.3 foal crop) were able to earn their stakes honors at major tracks in important races.

The champions also came regularly, especially the juveniles, and it is fair to say that the 1960s in North American racing circles belonged to Bold Ruler. He was, truly, the most dominant stallion over a single decade ever seen in America, at least since racing statistics have been maintained in an organized fashion.

The list of champions or major stakes winners during that time was overwhelming: Lamb Chop, Bold Lad (both American and Irish versions), Queen Empress, Bold Bidder, Gamely, Successor, Vitriolic, and Queen of the Stage, all year-end champions; and Bold Hour, Cornish Prince, What a Pleasure, Batteur, Great Power, Boldnesian, Bold Experience, Chieftain, Bold Commander, Irish Castle, King Emperor, Stupendous, and Reviewer among the many high-class non-champions.

Sometimes, they seemed to come in waves, and it was not easy to find a major stake race, especially for two-year-olds, without a Bold something or other in the field.

Despite his enormous successes and the great demand for his services, Bold Ruler was never syndicated, and his book sizes were kept in line with what

Bull Hancock and the Phipps family felt was prudent. His largest foal crop was thirty-five, and he sired only 356 named foals in thirteen crops, an average of 27.38 foals per class.

At the end of the sixties, Bold Ruler was unquestionably the king of the American stallion hill. The knock against him — and there is always a knock — was that he had never sired the winner of a Triple Crown race and, correspondingly, not many of his best offspring were up to winning at a mile and a quarter or more. Further, many of those brilliant young horses did not even get to the classics, often due to infirmities that compromised their careers.

Bold Lad and Reviewer were excellent examples of the Bold Ruler "problem." Both were high-class two-year-olds, flashed brief but good form at three (Bold Lad was, in fact, injured in the 1965 Kentucky Derby), and were outstanding in abbreviated four-year-old seasons.

With his career in its latter stages, the question had become this: Would this marvelous stallion, who had set perhaps unreachable standards for future stallions, fade into the twilight with the footnote that he could not get a classic winner or high-class stayer?

The question took on increased urgency when, in the summer of 1970, Bold Ruler was found to have a large, malignant tumor near his brain that was causing him breathing difficulties. He would travel to Auburn University for experimental cobalt treatments that succeeded in arresting the growth of the cancer, but it was clear, at age seventeen this grand horse had little time left.

He would stand one more season, but the cancer had returned by late spring of 1971. Bold Ruler was euthanized in July of that year, a few months after Gladys Phipps, his breeder and owner, had died.

There were more Bold Rulers still on the production line, but could any of them do what so many good ones had not done?

CHAPTER 3

Raising The Curtain

When a proven, world-class mare is in foal to a stallion of similar reputation, hopes and expectations are always high, and, by 1970, any prospective Bold Ruler foal would be the object of much attention. With Sir Gaylord off to a promising start at stud, and Bold Ruler in the twilight of his great career, the Meadow Stud connections were hopeful of an outcome from the Bold Ruler-Somethingroyal coin flip mating that would have a long-term impact on the Meadow operation.

The foal that was the tangible result of that coin flip in Alfred Vanderbilt's office was conceived on April 20, 1969, in the Claiborne Farm breeding shed, only yards away from Bold Ruler's stall. After being bred, Somethingroyal stayed at Claiborne with her filly foal (The Bride) from the previous season's mating to Bold

Ruler until shortly after the filly was weaned, then headed back home to The Meadow.

There, shortly after midnight on March 30, 1970, she produced a colt, a big one, without complications, according to farm records. Unlike his sire or dam, both bays, the colt was a chestnut. His coat was splashed heavily with white (again, unlike Mom or Dad), with white stockings well up both hind legs and halfway to the knee on his right foreleg and with a prominent star on his forehead with a slender stripe dwindling toward his nose.

He was well and powerfully made, a really handsome and impressive youngster, almost too pretty had it not been for his substance.

Secretary Elizabeth Ham's farm log carried a recording from July 28, 1970, four months after the big guy's birth:

Ch.C Bold Ruler—Somethingroyal
Three white stockings — Well-made colt —
Might be a little light under the knees —
Stands well on pasterns — Good straight
hind leg — Good shoulders and hindquar-
ters — You have to like him.

The Meadow's key staff, including farm manager

Howard Gentry and Bob Bailes, who ran The Meadow's training operation and would be responsible for teaching the 1970 Meadow babies their initial race-track lessons, shared Ham's assessment.

In the fall of 1970, the chestnut colt was weaned from Somethingroyal, by then in foal to First Landing. Even more impressive as a weanling, the colt needed a fitting name. Ham sent a list of possibilities to The Jockey Club in late fall.

The first three names were rejected as already in use, as were the first two on the second list. The other names, in order of submission, were Scepter, Royal Line, Something Special, Games of Chance, and Deo Volente (a Latin term for "God willing"). Approval came for the sixth name submitted, one Ham herself picked from a previous career association. The name was Secretariat.

The strapping chestnut colt now had a name and an unusually strong appetite. He was playful and boisterous with his fellow yearlings in the paddocks, enjoying the bumping and running and miniature skirmishes that are part of the carefree life of a young Thoroughbred.

Placed in the most prominent stall in The Meadow's yearling barn, Secretariat had an uneventful year from weaning to training time, with no illnesses or injuries beyond the normal nicks that young horses acquire.

The Meadow staff worked closely with its youngsters but gave them lots of time to develop. Secretariat thrived in that environment, showing an aggressive character blended with a good disposition and unusual intelligence. He was so attractive that The Meadow's employees found themselves hoping, almost praying, that this one might live up to his breeding and looks. The farm and racing stable needed a boost, given the uncertainties surrounding Chris Chenery's health and the possible disposition of the operation if he died.

In the summer of 1971, when Secretariat was in racing kindergarten, The Meadow's first major racehorse since Sir Gaylord and Cicada emerged, offering hope nearer on the horizon.

A bay colt by First Landing, he was named Riva Ridge (after a ridge near the Tweedys' ski-resort home in Vail, Colorado; the Colorado ridge was, in turn, named for a World War II battle site in Italy where

Tweedy had fought.) Though he lacked Secretariat's picture-book appearance, he was poetry in motion.

Riva Ridge was lanky and lop-eared, with a wiry muscle structure and cat-like quickness. He could run and carry his speed well enough to win seven of his nine starts in the summer and fall of 1971, earn more than $500,000, and get himself named North American champion two-year-old male. Going into winter quarters, he looked like a colt capable of becoming a classic horse and was solidly favored for the 1972 Derby.

Back at the farm, Secretariat was growing steadily into an eye-catching specimen as he and his Meadow stablemates prepared to join the racing stable in Florida. He was big, strong, a bit on the plump side, and moved gracefully for a colt of his bulk.

Conformationally, racing people compared him with his sire and the many Bold Rulers that had displayed their talents on American tracks. Bold Ruler was leggy, clean-limbed, with wonderfully straight hind legs and the sloping croup (rump) typical of Nearco-line horses. He was long-bodied, more so than Nasrullah and most of his sons, and a bit narrower as well. His only unattractive feature was a Roman-like head, which made him look more common than his body type suggested.

Secretariat was a lot like Bold Ruler, and more. Wider in front, with a powerful chest, he appeared to be shorter backed, perhaps because of his huskier frame, and he shared his sire's superb back end. Oh, and he had a head to kill for, plus that gorgeous copper coat.

In other words, he looked the part. But, could he play it?

The early returns were mixed.

Bob Bailes had repeatedly schooled The Meadow's yearlings in company on the farm's one-mile training track, so they were already used to galloping alongside each other, occasionally brushing lightly as the exercise riders accustomed them to running in groups.

Secretariat easily did what he was asked, seemingly enjoying the atmosphere and the minor jostling during morning gallops. Unlike Bold Ruler, whose early bursts of speed at Hialeah as a youngster had observers shaking their heads in wonderment, Secretariat was work-manlike. Not bad, but not exceptional.

The prior summer Roger Laurin had taken over

training the powerful Phipps stable, handing over the Meadow Stable reins to his father, Lucien, who was known as a genial but tougher taskmaster, a capable horseman for whom preparation was everything.

The capable Canadian rider Ron Turcotte, who rode regularly for Lucien Laurin and was Riva Ridge's pilot, sometimes galloped Secretariat. Turcotte liked Secretariat's affable demeanor and his way of going, but, like others in the Meadow Stable entourage, including those back at the farm, wondered if the youngster would outgrow the baby fat and learn to use that big frame in racehorse style.

Secretariat's early breezes gave everyone pause. Although he generally stayed up with his classmates going two or three furlongs, he found himself trailing on more than one occasion as the distance lengthened. He was a push-button ride, easily controllable, unlike many of his companions, but seemingly unsure about what to do when the tempo increased.

If bumped, he would bump back, as if playing a game, but he did not get aggressive and strain to accelerate as Laurin and Turcotte would have preferred. A typical Bold Ruler he was not.

Riva Ridge, meanwhile, started his three-year-old season with a sparkling win in the Hibiscus Stakes at Hialeah and then was upset in the Everglades as Turcotte got him trapped and never found room to run. Laurin was livid with Turcotte but shipped the colt to Kentucky for the Blue Grass Stakes at Keeneland, giving Turcotte a chance at redemption.

In the Blue Grass Stakes at Keeneland, Riva was his normal self, taking the lead quickly and winning easily, his impressive performance boosting him to Kentucky Derby favorite.

At that time the Blue Grass was still being run on a Thursday, only nine days before the Derby, and Riva Ridge carried his Keeneland form directly to Churchill Downs. He ran a race reminiscent of the Blue Grass and won almost as easily, giving Meadow Stable its first Derby victory after thirty-six years of playing the game at a high level. National television cameras focused on Penny Tweedy for the first time. Her charm and sincerity won her, and her family's horse, lots of fans.

The Preakness, unfortunately, was not so happy. Faced with a wet racetrack, Riva Ridge was lapped on

Key to the Mint, thought to be his toughest opponent, while a longshot named Bee Bee Bee bowled along on the lead.

Bee Bee Bee won handily over Derby runner-up No Le Hace, with Riva Ridge fourth, a neck behind Key to the Mint. Turcotte said Riva Ridge didn't like the race-track, but privately Laurin and Tweedy didn't like Turcotte, or at least his ride in the Preakness, but decided to stay with him for the Belmont in three weeks.

Back in New York, Riva Ridge and his jockey were dominant in the mile and a half third leg of the Triple Crown. The race was almost a duplicate of the Derby, with Riva Ridge leading almost the entire race, clipping off steady quarter miles in twenty-four seconds or so, coming home virtually alone (a seven-length margin) in 2:28, then the third fastest time in Belmont history.

Riva Ridge looked so good that Tweedy and Laurin decided to ship to California for the Swaps Stakes. There, Riva Ridge would have to carry 129 pounds under the race's allowance conditions, going a mile and a quarter, only three weeks after the Belmont. For a horse of his front-running style, this was asking a lot. Riva Ridge managed to do what was asked of him, but was hard pressed and came home a worthy but tired third.

The Swaps, unfortunately, probably because of its proximity to the Triple Crown regimen, took more out of the Meadow star than anyone recognized. He would lose his final five starts of the year, and by late fall it was evident he wasn't the same horse he had been earlier.

While Riva Ridge was on the classics trail, his year-younger stablemate had been finally showing signs that he might — perhaps, at last — be learning how to get out of his own way.

In mid-April, Secretariat and apprentice jockey/exercise rider Paul Feliciano headed to Belmont Park's training track for a morning gallop. A few minutes later Secretariat was standing alone at the gap leading to the stable area, having left Feliciano face down in the mud after the colt shied away from a horse approaching from the rear.

While only Feliciano's pride was wounded, Secretariat came back with strained back muscles that would keep him away from serious exercise for a couple of weeks. When Secretariat had mended, he had a new exercise rider in Jimmy Gaffney, a mutuel teller in the afternoon who had worked for Laurin several years earlier, galloping horses in the mornings. The colt returned at what turned out to be a propitious moment.

Gaffney immediately fell in love with his new partner, telling Laurin and anyone else who would listen that Secretariat was a star in the making. He liked the way the colt moved, his common sense, and his remarkable strength.

For the first time, too, the youngster was beginning to show some dash in his morning workouts, catching the eye of the Daily Racing Form clockers whose job it is to record workout times for their publication and to comment on anything they regard as exceptional.

Secretariat's times and his stride were starting to get footnotes on the Racing Form workout pages. Laurin had put blinkers on him in early June for his workouts, hoping to improve the colt's concentration, and the tactic seemed to be helping. Six furlongs in 1:12 4/5 on June 24 and three furlongs in :35 a few days later had him primed, as far as the *Form*'s handicappers were concerned, for his debut in a maiden special weight event (for non-winners of a race, carrying level weights).

That race came on Independence Day, 1972, at Aqueduct, and the bettors, who could both read a pedigree line and recognize good looks when they saw them, made Secretariat a 3.10-1 favorite.

The curtain was about to rise.

CHAPTER 4

Champion Among Champions

Racing fans at Aqueduct on July 4, 1972, had to love Secretariat's looks, unless they were those who think chestnuts, especially those with lots of white on their legs and heads, are best seen on posters and not in stretch drives.

They also had to love his pedigree, unless they were Bold Ruler skeptics (can't win a classic, won't go a mile and a quarter, too brittle to make it through the Triple Crown grind, etc.).

Likewise, those onlookers at Aqueduct had to love his connections. The Meadow was a leading private breeder operation with a lengthy record of producing good-class horses. The Canadian-born Lucien Laurin, at age sixty, had trained a number of nice ones since leaving behind riding for training in the early 1940s. Among them were the champion filly Quill, 1966

Belmont Stakes winner Amberoid, and Claiborne's talented homebred Dike, who was unfortunate to be a three-year-old in 1969, the same year as Majestic Prince and Arts and Letters.

But while Jimmy Gaffney might have fallen in love with Secretariat at first sight or during their first gallop together, Penny Tweedy, Lucien Laurin, and others in the Meadow Stable entourage still were not ready to commit their hearts.

Secretariat's size concerned Laurin, who saw potential under the colt's baby fat but worried about the colt's ability to withstand the training regimen necessary to get him fit for racing. Then, there was Secretariat's propensity to clown when working with other horses, his tendency to duck and dive and wander in search of a workmate to bump.

Secretariat liked to play, he loved to eat, but it wasn't clear at the threshold of his two-year-old season that he wanted to run or understood any of what was expected of him. The steady improvement in his morning workout times came more as a relief to Penny Tweedy than as a revelation. Perhaps he was going to be more than just a lovely, happy-go-lucky hunk. Tweedy, preoccupied with Riva Ridge's Triple Crown efforts, relied on Laurin's reports about Secretariat's progress, and Laurin's words were more reassuring than revealing. It was not until June 24, when Secretariat worked six furlongs in 1:12 4/5, that Laurin told Tweedy that the colt was ready to run and that, yes, he thought she should be in town for his first start.

One thing was clear: Secretariat was not a typical Bold Ruler. Maybe precocity had skipped a generation. Still, the clockers had begun to notice his improvement, and with that pedigree, he had enormous potential.

Partnered with Paul Feliciano, the same rider he had left face down on Belmont's training track almost three months earlier, Secretariat went to the races for the first time.

The day was cloudy, the temperature in the mid-seventies, unusually moderate for Independence Day. Eleven other two-year-olds were in the field of the five-and-a-half furlong race for non-winners, five of them with previous racing experience.

Juvenile maiden races are horse racing's ultimate handicapping challenge because so little is known about the participants, even by their trainers and riders. Bettors tend to focus on pedigrees and particulars such as the trainer's reputation with young horses or the consistency of workouts, knowing that none of these things mean much when the starting gates open.

Secretariat's slight favoritism in his debut was, undoubtedly, a result of his sire, his kinship to Sir Gaylord, the stable's recent successes, and his physical appearance. What else was there?

Feliciano and his mount were loaded into post position two without incident, and when New York starter George Cassidy sent the field away at 2:02 p.m. (plus thirty seconds), they broke in good order.

For about three strides.

A colt named Quebec, who was in post position four, ducked in abruptly, slamming into Secretariat from the right. Quebec's sideways lunge forced back Strike the Line, in post position three, and knocked Secretariat to his left, where he bumped Big Burn, the inside horse, who bounced back against the Meadow colt. For a few seconds, Secretariat was trapped between Quebec and Big Burn, each leaning on him. He staggered, almost going to his knees, then regained his footing and began to chase his field.

Initially, Secretariat made modest progress, seeming unsure of what he was supposed to do. Laurin, not having seen the incident at the start, prepared to shoot Feliciano on sight. He was angry a colt that had trained well at the starting gate got away so slowly.

Feliciano, for his part, looked for a place to send the colt, who began to pick up his pace. Midway through Aqueduct's final turn, he couldn't find a clear path and bumped another horse slightly while trying to slide outside. He then dipped inside turning for home, finally locating some racing room.

With less than a quarter mile to run, Secretariat was seventh, about six lengths behind, out of contention. By mid-stretch, he was closing fast, cutting down the leaders' margins with each stride.

He was rolling as the finish neared, only to have his path along the rail blocked as the field neared the finish line. Although Feliciano had to ease him back just before the wire due to the traffic ahead, they finished a surging fourth, beaten about a length and a quarter by the winner, Calumet Farm's Herbull.

Feliciano anticipated Laurin's tirade, which occurred as the jockey weighed out near Aqueduct's trackside paddock. Soon, however, Laurin saw the race replay and realized what had occurred at the start. He not only apologized to Feliciano, but had confirmation that the big, lumbering chestnut clown of a few months ago was about to become a real racehorse, one that should have won his first start.

Laurin wasted no time in throwing Secretariat — and Feliciano — back into the pool, entering the colt in another maiden race, this one at six furlongs, on July 15, again at Aqueduct.

Secretariat seemed unfazed by his brush with race-track mayhem. His appetite remained healthy, and he worked out in good order. The *Racing Form* chartcallers and clockers wrote in a post-race mortem that he was an unlucky loser with good things in front of him.

Joined by ten other maidens in the post parade for his second start, Secretariat had the attention of the bettors, who made him the solid favorite at 1.30-1. Feliciano felt even more pressure not to let this one get away.

Although Secretariat broke alertly enough, he dropped back quickly, slow to get into stride. Feliciano, not wanting to panic and to rush him, decided to let him find his best stride on his own.

That seemed to take some time, and Laurin was seeing his worst nightmare being played out again. The colt couldn't, or wouldn't, maintain contact with his field, and Feliciano seemed powerless to get him going.

Then, without pressure from his jockey, Secretariat decided to enter the race. Staying well away from the inside rail, he powered forward, hauling Feliciano with him as if the jockey were an inert passenger, strapped on for a rocket ride. The pair flew by everyone else, drawing away to win by six widening lengths in an impressive 1:10 3/5 for the six furlongs, with Master Achiever, who had finished second in Secretariat's first start, again second.

Now, thought Tweedy and Laurin, that was more like it.

Charlie Hatton, the elder statesman of American racing writers, was on the Secretariat story quickly. Chief columnist for the *Daily Racing Form*, Hatton had been studying Thoroughbreds for six decades. Unlike many members of his profession, Hatton had a practiced eye. He was trained at an early age by instinctive horsemen and honed by seeing virtually every top racehorse produced in America from World War I onward. Hatton could turn a phrase with the best, never more so than when he was describing a favorite horse.

Hatton got his first close-up look at Secretariat in the paddock at horse racing's version of Mecca, Saratoga Race Course, and his subsequent commentary on the colt bore the signature of a man smitten.

The man who had nurtured the Triple Crown with his prose, made the Triple Crown a common term in Thoroughbred racing's lexicon, chronicled the feats of dozens of wonderful racehorses over a lengthy and distinguished career, was, in his sunset years, head over heels in love, and with a red-headed two-year-old who had won but a single race.

Racehorses have a way of humbling their admirers, both with their virtuosity and their vulnerability. Racing writers learn, at their peril, to be guarded in their praise of even the most accomplished of horses, and Hatton, while more florid and flattering than most, knew how to temper his testimonials.

Except with Secretariat. Readers of the *Racing Form* would note that Hatton made several references to the colt even before the colt had won his second race. Secretariat had to be one of the most talked about non-winners of two races in history.

That second win came on July 31, 1972, at Saratoga, in a race for non-winners of two races, over six furlongs, and Secretariat was facing six others, including previous winners.

His pilot this time was primary stable jockey Ron Turcotte, who had been busy winning the Monmouth Oaks aboard Rokeby Stable's Summer Guest when Secretariat debuted, and then had been recuperating from a fall when the colt broke his maiden. Feliciano continued to ride for Laurin as a second stringer.

Laurin told Turcotte he should be ready for Secretariat's race at Saratoga on July 31, and, injury aside, the jockey was true to his word.

Although facing better competition, the Meadow youngster ran a race similar to his last outing, this time as odds-on favorite at .40-1. Laurin had decided that Secretariat wanted to run leisurely in the early stages of his races, so he advised Turcotte to let the colt find his own stride.

Secretariat broke reasonably, and then dropped back to last, getting himself comfortable with the pace. Turcotte allowed him to bowl along as he pleased. The rider's job with horses that like to settle in the back of the field and make their bid as they please is to find a route uncluttered by other equine traffic.

Turcotte decided that the overland route was safest. He sent his fellow wide on the turn, giving up a lot of ground but also providing Secretariat a clear path in the stretch. His mount then did what 2-5 shots are supposed to. He swept by the erstwhile leaders and drew away to an uneasy, unpressured one and a half-length win, the six furlongs run in 1:10 4/5.

Secretariat's race had not been scintillating, but it could also not be faulted. He had run it his way and had looked very professional in doing so. The fact that he was no tear-away, having to be in front or be nowhere, augured well for both his longevity and his ability to travel routinely the longer distances over which his sire's offspring were thought to be suspect.

Secretariat and Turcotte next ventured into stakes company with a run at the Sanford Stakes on August 16. The Sanford should probably be renamed The Only Race Man o' War Ever Lost Stakes, since it is invariably referred to that way. That historical anomaly aside, it is also a meaningful prep for Saratoga's most prestigious juvenile event, the Hopeful Stakes.

The Sanford of 1972 would get special attention, partly because it represented the stakes coming-out party for Charlie Hatton's "perfect horse," and also because Secretariat would be facing a legitimate talent in Linda's Chief, a son of the Bold Ruler stallion Chieftain and winner of five straight races.

Saratoga's horseplayers were not as willing as Hatton and other racing professionals to send Secretariat directly into the Racing Hall of Fame across Union Avenue from the track. They made Linda's Chief the 3-5 favorite, with the Meadow star-in-waiting at 3-2, reasoning that Linda's Chief had more experience against better competition and a handier running style, perhaps better in a six-furlong race.

Five two-year-olds lined up facing starter George Cassidy for the Sanford, but in reality, three were out for some late-afternoon exercise. Those expecting a match race would be disappointed, however, for Secretariat never let it happen. He took his usual stroll through the first three furlongs or so, trailing the leader, Trevose, by about four lengths as they made the bend for the stretch.

As Secretariat got in gear, two horses blocked him in the early stretch, with Linda's Chief positioned perfectly outside of him, away from any trouble. Turcotte decided to go between the leaders, testing his horse's courage and competitive spirit.

The big chestnut would not be found wanting in either category. He blasted through a narrow gap and sped away to a three-length victory that looked wider, running six furlongs in 1:10, equaling the fastest time of the Saratoga meeting.

The Sanford made him the clear leader of his division. It also made him the class bully and the emerging glamour boy of American racing. He was pretty, he was a he-man, he could run, and he was a relaxed, happy camper away from the track. Secretariat was a dream come true.

His reputation only whetted the appetites of trainers, who live for the opportunity to expose the chinks in the latest hero's armor.

Thus, the Hopeful, on August 26, drew eight entries willing to test Secretariat over six and a half furlongs. Everything about the colt suggested that he would race better as the distances lengthened, but skeptics were already reminding everyone that his powerful conformation, as splendid as it was, hinted more at speed than stamina and, besides, he was a Bold Ruler.

The Hopeful has been won by many standout horses, including future champions, classic winners, leading sires, and Hall of Famers. Its timing now makes it more of a mid-season all-star game, a prelude to the climactic juvenile races of the fall, signifying that it is time to get serious.

The 1972 Hopeful, arrayed with nice horses like Stop the Music, Step Nicely, and Torsion, each of whom would prove to be a quality performer, looked like a typical running of the race.

Secretariat, unaware of history or his competition, simply did what he was accustomed to doing, breaking from the gate and settling behind the other eight starters while trying to find his rhythm down Saratoga's backside.

Turcotte, by now used to the style, let him do as he pleased, waiting until he felt his horse pick up the bit and gather momentum before seeking a runway for takeoff.

The colt was surging so smoothly and powerfully on

his own that Turcotte decided to steer him away from the others and, as the *Racing Form* chart comment said, he "looped his field on the turn." This dramatically understated what happened, for Secretariat had literally gone from last to first in a little over an eighth of a mile. He did this in :22 or less, an incredible sprint on a turn, and he wasn't through. He powered his way through the stretch for a five-length win that could have been greater, running six and a half furlongs in 1:16 1/5, three-fifths of a second off the track record held by another handsome chestnut son of Bold Ruler out of a Princequillo mare, Bold Lad.

Away from the field of dreams, though, the news was not so good. Chris Chenery's health had deteriorated. At eighty-six his memory was gone. He weighed less than one hundred pounds, could not speak, and was constantly bedridden, unable to comprehend that he had bred another classic winner and champion in Riva Ridge and that a horse with the potential to be even better than Riva — perhaps the horse of a lifetime — was wearing his blue-and-white silks.

Beyond the emotional torment of watching their father slowly fade away, the Chenery siblings had to contemplate estate tax consequences upon his death. They would certainly have to sell or syndicate both Secretariat and Riva Ridge once Chris Chenery was gone, and timing would be critical.

Their desire, of course, would be to sell or syndicate when the horses' values were highest, but none of that could be predicted.

Also troubling was the sudden death of Bull Hancock who had left Saratoga for a hunting trip in Scotland not feeling well. The hunting trip was abbreviated, and Hancock flew home for an examination followed by exploratory surgery in late August. Doctors discovered advanced lung cancer, and Hancock died on September 14, 1972, leaving a void in his family, his farm, and in the lives of a multitude of clients and friends in the international racing community

Two days after Hancock's death, Secretariat ran in the Futurity at Belmont, an important stop on the road to the two-year-old championship. The race, in its eighty-third year, had been the pre-eminent American juvenile race until the late 1950s, when the Garden State Stakes and New York's own Champagne Stakes, longer and richer races, became more definitive tests.

At its inception the Futurity was America's richest race, which it remained for many years, and, like the Hopeful, had a lengthy list of distinguished winners, including Riva Ridge on his way to a two-year-old championship.

Secretariat blasted through a stupendous five-furlong workout in :58 the week of the Futurity and looked happy afterward, although Laurin worried the colt might have overdone it.

In retrospect he could have been correct. The colt, sent off as a 1-5 favorite, did not get a hold of the sandy Belmont surface as well as he had Saratoga's main track. Nonetheless, he made a strong move on the turn, drove to the lead in early stretch, then was tapped twice by Turcotte's whip to keep a resolute Stop the Music at bay by one and three-quarters lengths, stopping the teletimer at 1:16 2/5 for six and a half furlongs.

Whether it was the fast workout or something else, Secretariat had not been as impressive as he had been at Saratoga. Privately, Turcotte wondered whether his tiring in the Futurity indicated stamina limitations.

Next up was the Champagne Stakes, which by 1972 had become New York's most important two-year-old race after years of toiling in the shadows of the Futurity and Hopeful. The Champagne, with its modest purse, had been treated as a minor event suited for late-developing juveniles, though its distance and timing, a mile in mid-fall, were more likely to indicate future possibilities than were the shorter races.

Spurred by the competition from the Garden State Stakes, which attracted the nation's best two-year-olds as the world's richest race, New York officials bumped the purse of the Champagne to six figures in the late fifties. It quickly started attracting top fields.

The 1972 running had twelve starters, almost certainly because trainers wanted to test Secretariat's mettle over a mile or perhaps because the Futurity's competitive finish had given them pause, as it had Turcotte. Possibly, Secretariat was simply a sprinter, as unlikely as it seemed, or maybe he was feeling the wear and tear of six starts in three months. Maybe he had an as yet undetected physical problem.

Some remembered that Bold Ruler was often stiff and arthritic in his movements until thoroughly warmed up. Stories abounded that Sunny Jim Fitzsimmons had trained him on anti-inflammatory drugs through much of his career, and Secretariat's rear-end action was almost identical.

The Belmont Park crowd, in excess of 31,000, apparently shared some of the horsemen's skepticism, sending the red colt off at .70-1, despite a strong mile work of 1:37 ten days before the race. For the Champagne, Secretariat would be coupled with stable-mate Angle Light, trained by Laurin but owned by Edwin Whittaker.

A few months before, Angle Light easily bested Secretariat in the mornings, but now the game had changed. Angle Light had ability but no longer was thought to be in the same class as his shed row companion.

The rest of the field, though, certainly offered Secretariat's severest test so far. Stop the Music, Step Nicely, Linda's Chief, and Puntilla, all winners of valuable two-year-old stakes, would be in the hunt, along with some promising newcomers.

The post-race chart noted that Secretariat was "void of early foot," which is putting it kindly since he was trailing by almost thirteen lengths after a half-mile (Angle Light was leading through a rapid half in :45 1/5).

Secretariat had his rhythm by then. He gathered steam, aiming for the leaders. Stop the Music was staying with Secretariat, just to his inside, and Turcotte would say after the race that Stop the Music came out and bumped him a couple of times on the turn.

At that point the racing began in earnest. Linda's Chief and Puntilla were battling for the lead, with Secretariat and Stop the Music in hot pursuit, Step Nicely trying to rally.

Turcotte tapped Secretariat with the whip just as they passed the three-sixteenths pole, and the colt changed leads, bumping Stop the Music and pushing him into Linda's Chief.

Secretariat accelerated away under pressure from Turcotte, winning by two lengths over Stop the Music, running the mile in 1:35.

The stewards had noted the brief skirmish in the stretch and quickly posted the inquiry sign. Several minutes later, after talking with the riders and reviewing the videotape, they took down the inquiry sign and Secretariat's number, disqualifying him to second place behind Stop the Music.

The film patrol camera didn't lie; Secretariat had

done what he was accused of doing and would pay the required price. He had also run a powerful race, coming from far off the pace through crowded conditions to blast — maybe a bit too strongly — past the best two-year-olds in training.

His reputation was undamaged, and everyone at Belmont that day knew that the best horse had finished in front, even if he had — justifiably — lost in the steward's office.

Charlie Hatton had reasonably restrained his pen until just prior to the Champagne when he wrote of Secretariat: "His impact on the contemporary turf promises to be enormous, that of a Promethean hero who does it all."

After the Champagne, Hatton would write: "It has been complained that the application of the Rules of Racing generally in America is often reminiscent of the infinite convolutions of bureaucracy, marked by inconsistency, obfuscation and ambiguity.

"But the New York officials had no alternative under the rules. They saw their duty and they did it."

Hatton was certain, as was everyone else in attendance on Champagne Day, that Secretariat was the best horse in the race. Turcotte, in fact, felt it was Secretariat's best performance yet, one that gave the jockey, at least, confidence in the colt's ability to negotiate longer distances successfully. Already impressed with his red-coated companion, Turcotte emerged from the Champagne as a true believer.

Secretariat and Turcotte were now about to venture outside of New York for the first time. They were on the road to Laurel Park in Laurel, Maryland, best known as home of the Washington, D.C., International, America's first major grass race.

Laurel also hosted the Laurel Futurity and the Selima Stakes, two prestigious two-year-old races, the latter for fillies. Both races had a lengthy tradition, each being won by numerous top colts and fillies.

Secretariat arrived a few days early to settle in before the Futurity and get a serious workout over an unfamiliar surface. He went five-eighths of a mile in 1:00 three days before the race, a brisk work intended to put him on edge to face what was expected to be a small field, but one with some early speed.

His opponents again included Stop the Music and stablemate Angle Light, both of whom were there to see if Secretariat was vulnerable over the mile and one-sixteenth trip, although few horsemen seriously doubted his ability to handle the distance with ease after his Champagne performance.

On race day, October 28, rain left the racing strip sloppy. The good news was that Bold Rulers typically did well on wet dirt tracks; the bad news was that Secretariat had never raced over slop or mud and was not a typical Bold Ruler in style, which is to say he was not the front-running speed type that normally does well on an off track.

Laurel's fans, undeterred by his inexperience with wet footing, made him a 1-10 favorite as part of an entry with Angle Light and watched with anticipation as the red colt sought to repay their confidence.

The race turned out to be the easiest of Secretariat's young career. Parked in post position five in the six-horse field, Secretariat left the gate in his usual relaxed fashion, then dropped back to last as Turcotte eased him to the outside to avoid the slop in his face and find the smoothest path. After the opening quarter-mile, run in :22 4/5 by pacesetter Rocket Pocket, the pair was more than thirteen lengths off the lead and had improved their position only by a couple of lengths after the first half-mile, run in a strong :45 4/5.

Despite his bulk and his reaching, pounding stride, Secretariat again demonstrated an amazing propensity for delivering devastating moves on the turns. The colt had shown Turcotte that he could both relax and pick up momentum simultaneously, and he was on a roll by the time they swept into the final turn.

By mid-turn, he was only three lengths off the lead, and he ripped by both Rocket Pocket and second-place Whatabreeze as they turned into the stretch. Stop the Music had tried, in vain, to go with him at the moment of blast-off, but the Meadow colt was drawing steadily away, being urged only by Turcotte's voice and hands.

Secretariat won by eight easy lengths, stopping the teletimer in a stakes-record 1:42 4/5, only a fifth of a second off the track record. Noteworthy were both the speed and ease of his victory, coming on a sloppy track while taking the overland route. He could scarcely have won with more facility or more disdain for his competition.

Now that Maryland was safely conquered, one stone remained unturned, that of the New Jersey's

Garden State Stakes, the richest two-year-old race in the world in its day.

When, in 1953, Garden State Park owner Eugene Mori upped the purse of the race to record levels and positioned it to be the final major juvenile contest of the year, his plan was met with skepticism within the racing industry. By giving away so much money in the Garden State and its filly counterpart, the Gardenia Stakes, Mori was trying to attract the best two-year-olds in training and make his track the championship stop for juveniles.

Some thought the races were novelties that would never last and certainly would not attract the top colts and fillies to the southern Jersey track, but they were wrong. Demonstrating once more that money talks louder than tradition or naysayers, the races were instant, and sustaining, hits.

The 1972 Garden State Stakes was run on November 18, twenty-one days after the Laurel Futurity, for a purse of $298,665, with $179,199 to the winner.

Secretariat went to Garden State Park early, with Laurin watching a small splint (a bony growth caused by the stress of running) that had developed on Secretariat's right front leg. He felt the splint was not yet bothering the colt, but a slow workout (he breezed six furlongs in 1:18 or thereabouts, far too leisurely for his trainer) on November 5 did concern Laurin. He worried not because of the splint but because this was a horse that now required hard, fast drills to keep him fit and alert.

Accordingly, he sent Secretariat seven furlongs in 1:25 4/5 on November 9 under Turcotte, then sent him on a quick three-furlong trip four days before the Garden State Stakes.

Secretariat and Angle Light were again coupled as the 1-10 favorites, although they were facing Step Nicely and Garden State trial winner Impecunious, along with Knightly Dawn and Venezuelan import Piamem.

Chopped liver this was not, but Secretariat treated his five rivals as if they weren't much better.

He did his usual number early: break cleanly but routinely, settle in the back of the field, and warm up for a furious finale. Secretariat trailed the leader, Piamem, who was just ahead of Angle Light, by ten lengths down the backside while they set a modest pace (:24 1/5 first quarter; :47 2/5 half-mile).

That moderate pace could have been his undoing, but the big chestnut was about to switch on his final-turn afterburners and when he did, the race was effectively over. He sailed by Impecunious and had dead aim on the leading Angle Light in early stretch, mowing him down almost casually and finishing on top by three and a half lengths, getting the mile and one-sixteenth trip in 1:44 2/5, with minimal urging by Turcotte.

That would be a wrap for 1972, and a remarkable year it had been. Secretariat's official tally was seven wins, one second, and one fourth in nine starts, with $456,404 in earnings.

His smashing fall, coming as Riva Ridge's sparkling season collapsed, pushed Meadow Stable to $1,171,207 in earnings, its best year ever, at a time when the racing stable and farm desperately needed it.

Only a few days after his Garden State victory, Secretariat was shipped to Hialeah, where his splint was pin-fired in early December. The colt began galloping again by late December, with expectations that he would start his Triple Crown pursuit in Florida later in the winter.

Secretariat was a strong winter-book favorite for the Kentucky Derby already, and his following only grew more intense when he became the first two-year-old ever selected as Horse of the Year in the combined year-end polls of the National Turf Writers Association, the Thoroughbred Racing Associations (racetrack trade group association), and the *Daily Racing Form* staff. (The polls were first combined in 1972 to create the Eclipse Awards as the official year-end championships.) Native Dancer in 1952 and the filly Moccasin in 1965 were the only two-year-olds ever to get a mention as Horse of the Year, and they won only the Thoroughbred Racing Associations poll.

There was some controversy over selecting a two-year-old over horses that had raced against broader competition, but Riva Ridge's competitive collapse cost him the three-year-old championship, won by Key to the Mint. Older star Autobiography had pummeled both Riva Ridge and Key to the Mint in the Jockey Club Gold Cup. Their inconsistencies had opened the door for racing's new glamour guy, and he took full advantage of it.

Charlie Hatton's description of his newest equine hero in his year-end profiles of 1972's leading horses in the *American Racing Manual* was remarkable for its incredibly detailed analysis of Secretariat's physique.

Hatton's admiration, or perhaps amazement, at what he had seen in the handsome son of Bold Ruler and Somethingroyal, his size, massive bone structure, powerful hindquarters, placid demeanor, and stunning power knew no literary bounds. Here was a two-year-old, already 16.1 hands tall, with the body of a mature horse, racing like an old pro, belying the views of the naysayers who suspected him of being a sprinter. They groused about his choppy, abrupt way of going until warmed up and traded rumors about his soundness.

Hatton wrote: "Whatever his future — a tour de force of vile luck — Secretariat has begun his career as a champion among champions.

"There was an unwritten guarantee of high drama whenever he sported the blue and white Chenery blocks. His incredible bursts of speed, transforming imminent defeat into triumph, were quite the hit of the '72 season on our turf."

Hatton would tell friends that he had seen no horse

like this since Man o' War, or perhaps ever. He was consumed with the colt.

To put a period on his year, Secretariat was given 129 pounds on the Experimental Free Handicap, the year-end theoretical weighting of the season's best two-year-olds. It was not the highest such weighting ever — Count Fleet was assigned 132 and Chance Sun, Bimelech, Alsab, Native Dancer, and Bold Lad were all given 130 — but it was unusually lofty, certifying the high regard for Secretariat among racing professionals and adding to expectations that exceeded even those held for Native Dancer as he turned three.

Could the twenty-five-year Triple Crown drought finally be about to end, and would a son of the most phenomenal stallion of his era, but one without a classic winner, be the one to provide relief?

The fat, happy pretty boy of spring had become a breathtaking, gorgeous sculpture, wonderfully made and even more talented. The early fears that he would be just another attractive failure had been swept away on the wings of consuming hope and expectations.

For the Meadow Stable team, the year would end on a wonderfully high note, with Secretariat being named champion two-year-old male as well as Horse of the Year, Laurin leading trainer, and The Meadow as leading owner and breeder.

Three days into the new year, all that would be momentarily set aside when Chris Chenery died.

Now, a new high-stakes drama was about to be played out, but with the scene shifting from the race-track to offices and boardrooms around the world.

CHAPTER 5

Syndication

The death of Chris Chenery brought both sadness and relief to his children. Gone was the patriarch who had raised a strong family and built a business empire and a lifelong dream, The Meadow. There was, however, relief that the ravages of illness and decline that had left him a shell were over. He was buried in Virginia, home at last, and his family and friends gathered at The Meadow to pay him homage.

For sisters Penny Tweedy and Margaret Carmichael and brother Hollis Chenery, this was a time not only for mourning but also for determining if Chris Chenery's beloved family estate could be preserved.

Estate taxes would be severe, and options ranged from total liquidation of the farm and its horses to a dispersal sale of the broodmare band and maybe even the unthinkable, the sale of Riva Ridge and Secretariat.

Clearly, if the farm was to survive, assets would have to be sold, and those assets would have to be valuable enough to pay the substantial taxes that would be levied.

To help evaluate their situation, the family hired Humphrey and John Finney, the chairman and president, respectively, of Fasig-Tipton Inc., the Thoroughbred auction house based in New York, with operations in major racing centers throughout the country. The Finneys and Fasig-Tipton also offered equine consulting, appraisal, and advisory services and were experienced in dealing with estate matters.

Penny Tweedy did not want to disperse The Meadow breeding and racing operations, although she knew some things would have to be sold to pay the estate taxes. Her goals were to preserve the farm, keep the best horses, if possible, and hold onto both Riva Ridge and Secretariat, at least for racing purposes.

She had thoughts about eventually standing both horses in Virginia, but John Finney dissuaded her. He told her he believed Riva Ridge to be worth about $2.5 million, but that the horse could, with a good four-year-old season, push that value up to between four million dollars and four and a half million dollars.

Secretariat, he believed, was worth between five million dollars and seven million dollars. Should he win the Triple Crown, his worth could rise another two million dollars, Finney said. If he failed to win all three legs, his value could decline three million dollars.

They discussed the "Bold Ruler problem," that is, the stallion's failure to sire a classic winner and the inability of several of his most promising sons even to make the Triple Crown races. Secretariat had been robust thus far, the minor splint late in his two-year-old season aside, but his size and powerful ground-pounding action raised concerns he was more likely to hurt himself in training or racing than the more fluid Riva Ridge. Having Bold Ruler as his sire only added to that concern.

After exploring their options, John Finney said the family should syndicate Secretariat now, before his three-year-old campaign, capitalizing on his Horse of the Year status, his looks, and his pedigree.

Based on Finney's valuation, the Chenery siblings decided to seek up to $200,000 for breeding shares in Secretariat and asked Claiborne Farm to arrange the deal.

Stallion syndication had, in a sense, been around for a long time, with stallion managers like Bull Hancock's father, A.B. Hancock Sr., getting small groups of prominent horsemen to form partnerships to buy young stallions such as Sir Gallahad III and Blenheim II, two of Claiborne's foundation sires.

The first modern syndicate, though, with a large number of shareholders acquiring permanent rights, was that of Beau Pere, the Australian horse owned by movie kingpin Louis B. Mayer and syndicated to stand in Kentucky by Leslie Combs II of Spendthrift Farm fame.

Combs and the Hancocks led the way in stallion syndications through the 1950s and 1960s, acquiring many of the world's top stallion prospects along the way. Others sometimes entered the fray, but Claiborne and/or Spendthrift rarely let a good one escape.

Secretariat, even at this stage in his career, was a tempting prize for a stallion operation, and the Chenery family decided to offer the syndication job to Claiborne because of its great tradition, lengthy list of blue-ribbon clients (i.e., great mares), and longtime connections to Chris Chenery's breeding operation.

This proved to be the first serious test for twenty-three-year-old Seth Hancock, who had succeeded his father as the head of Claiborne after an all-too-brief apprenticeship following college. The young Hancock loved the farm and the horses and had long known what he wanted to do with his life. He joined Claiborne full-time in early 1972, expecting to spend years learning from his father and the staff.

Half a year later the sudden death of his father shattered those plans. Now, a year after becoming part of the Claiborne operation, he not only was in charge but was being asked to syndicate a horse for more money than anyone else had ever sought, a horse who had just turned three, with his most serious racing still in front of him.

Hancock reached an agreement with Tweedy and her attorney whereby the horse would be syndicated into thirty-two shares, twenty-eight to be sold (the estate would keep four) at $190,000 per share for a record total of $6,080,000. The colt would race, all being well, in the Triple Crown and other major events and retire to Claiborne by November 15, 1973. He would race under full control of Meadow Stable, which would assume all liabilities and would determine his racing schedule.

Immediate retirement was considered, but both Tweedy and Hancock said it would be better to race Secretariat at three. They also supported an ambitious schedule outlined by Laurin that included the Triple Crown and major races in the fall.

Secretariat, meanwhile, was training in Florida like the star he already was, although Tweedy and Hancock had agreed the colt would not race until the syndication was completed. He worked five-eighths of a mile in :58 3/5 on February 7, six furlongs in 1:11 2/5 on February 12, and seven furlongs in 1:23 2/5 on February 28, with a couple of additional short, fast works interspersed. The workout on the last day in February, when he galloped out a mile in 1:35 4/5, inspired Laurin to tell a writer, "I knew right then he was one of the greatest horses I ever saw."

Original plans had included the Flamingo Stakes on March 3, but Laurin told Tweedy that the big chestnut youngster, who had grown since his juvenile year and was both more fluid and more aggressive in the mornings, would not be fit enough for the mile and one-eighth test, despite his string of "black-type" workouts.

Laurin advised Tweedy they needed to take the New York route to the Derby (the Bay Shore Stakes, Gotham Stakes, and Wood Memorial), a schedule that offered a progression of distances but left little margin for error.

Separately, John Finney, not knowing that Claiborne was about to mount a syndication effort, was in discussion with Irish breeder Captain A.D.D. "Tim" Rogers, master of Airlie Stud, and Irish agent Jonathan Irwin about buying Secretariat and eventually bringing him to Ireland for stud duty.

Tim Rogers had been a friend of Chris Chenery, and of Bull Hancock, and he had great respect for Claiborne's record as a maker of stallions. He had witnessed an array of good European horses make their way to Claiborne, horses like Nasrullah, Count Martial, Ambiorix, Herbager, and Le Fabuleux, as the Hancocks sought new bloodlines to cross with the many quality mares owned by the farm and its clients.

Rogers had also seen those European bloodlines exported after the two world wars come back in the form of American-breds competing in Europe, beginning in earnest in the mid-1960s, and doing so with astounding success. The American horses, a distillation of European and native American bloodlines, tested under tough American conditions, dominated international racing, and to Rogers, Secretariat was the perfect model.

Rogers and Irwin authorized Finney to make a $6.5 million offer, with the stipulation that Secretariat would eventually perform his stud duties in Ireland.

Penny Tweedy, with this offer in hand but a desire, if possible, to keep the horse that might save The Meadow in the land of his birth, told Seth Hancock to go ahead with the ambitious syndication effort.

Thus began one of the most unique episodes in the history of stallion syndications. While syndicating horses as young as Secretariat was not a rarity, the previous cases involved colts that had been injured after dazzling starts to their careers and would be unable to race again.

Selling shares in a healthy three-year-old who was favored to win the Kentucky Derby but had not yet started at three was unheard of, and even Secretariat's pedigree, race record, physique, and startling good looks were no guarantees of success.

Seth Hancock had two advantages as he prepared

for his nerve-wracking task: the first was the product he was selling; the second was the world's finest Rolodex of Thoroughbred breeders. Nobody would refuse a call from Claiborne, and the farm's long-term record would give comfort to those reservations about either Secretariat's prospects or the youth and inexperience of Seth Hancock.

His first call was to Ogden Phipps, who had lost Secretariat in the coin toss and was now part of a three-man committee advising Hancock on the management of Claiborne. Phipps, after a brief discussion, committed to a share in the spectacular son of Bold Ruler, the best stallion ever owned by Phipps' family.

Phipps could be expected to support the syndication effort, even at an eyebrow-raising price, but others were more skeptical as Hancock quoted the terms and conditions of the offer: ten percent down, forty percent when the colt passed a fertility test upon retirement, and the remaining fifty percent prior to the 1974 breeding season.

Some prospective shareholders inhaled as they heard the $190,000 price. A number of them had bought shares in the highest-priced syndicate ever, before this one, the $5.4 deal done by Claiborne on behalf of Nijinsky II in 1970 and that was for a horse who had won the English Triple Crown, the first horse to do so in thirty-five years.

Secretariat might have the same potential, but if he failed or got hurt or simply turned out to be a good but unremarkable three-year-old when asked to stretch out over longer distances, that $190,000 might take a very long time to recoup.

Hancock called an international list of clients, including some relative newcomers to Thoroughbred racing and a number of veteran Kentucky breeders.

Interestingly, perhaps predictably, it was the local breeders who gave him the most heartburn, possibly because they understood too well the risks of the breeding business and the ease with which one can fall in love with a horse.

Bill Nack, a gifted and versatile writer who for many years practiced his craft for *Sports Illustrated*, wrote an absorbing firsthand account of Secretariat's racing life, originally published in 1975 under the title *Big Red of Meadow Stable*, reprinted in 2002 as *Secretariat: the Making of a Champion*.

Nack devoted a couple of chapters to the quiet drama of the four days in February 1973, during which Seth Hancock calmly and diligently pushed the syndication of Secretariat through more than a few uncertain moments.

After one day, according to Nack's account, only six shares were sold, Greentree Stud and Virginia breeder Taylor Hardin had said no, and such established breeders as Allaire du Pont and Walter Salmon had said, "Maybe. I'll call you back. I need to think about it."

Seth Hancock didn't need to hear that sort of hesitancy from such well-established clients. This suggested that when balancing Secretariat's appeal against the unknowns, it was a tough call.

Gradually, with a few hiccups, the syndicate came together. Salmon and du Pont said yes, as did Will Farish, Paul Mellon, Warner Jones, Tartan Farm, Swiss banker Walter Haefner, French breeder Jacques Wertheimer, Canadian breeder-owner E.P. Taylor, Japanese breeder Zenya Yoshida, and Captain Tim Rogers, who learned, as a result of Hancock's call, that Secretariat's syndication was moving ahead and that he would not get the horse for his Irish farm.

Others who stepped up included Central Kentucky restaurant entrepreneur Dan Lasater, longtime Claiborne client Howard Keck, Pennsylvania horseman George Strawbridge, Virginia horseman Bert Firestone, paper manufacturer Howard Gilman, Widener family scion Eugene Dixon, and Alfred Vanderbilt, who got the last share when a buyer dropped out.

Seth Hancock had delivered the gift of time and money to the Chenery estate. Now it was up to Secretariat, soon on his way to New York for the Bay Shore Stakes at Aqueduct on March 17.

The syndication effort had accomplished what was necessary for The Meadow's immediate survival, but it placed enormous pressure on Tweedy, Laurin, Hancock, and Turcotte, all to be carried on the powerful shoulders of a three-year-old colt yet to make his first start of the year. Was he on the road to glory, or the path to oblivion?

CHAPTER 6

Derby Trail Disappointment

H ad Secretariat been endowed with a literary bent, he would have been both amused and amazed at what he read in the spring of 1973, and quite possibly would have felt burdened to the point of distraction by the level of expectation surrounding his every move. Racing writers, as well as sports commentators who rarely showed any interest in the sport of kings, were reporting on his workouts, his planned racing schedule, his health, and the various rumors and rumble that go with celebrity status.

In Florida, Laurin had made Secretariat's workouts lengthy enough to make demands on his respiratory capacity and fast enough to test every muscle fiber he possessed. The colt had eaten well and slept well, and a substantial workload had been necessary to keep him tight and enthusiastic. Now back in New York, his regimen was the same, or even more intense, as he drew close to racing.

On Wednesday, March 14, three days before his seasonal bow, Secretariat was out among the photographers, reporters, and numerous interested racetrackers for a three-furlong burst over Belmont Park's main track. Laurin now understood that Secretariat needed a fast workout close to the race to really get his attention.

Laurin wanted speed that morning at Belmont Park. He got even more than he bargained for, while everyone else got an eyeful. The colt galloped through his warm-up, then, at Turcotte's urging, leveled off at racing speed from the middle of the sweeping turn at Belmont through the finish line, a three-eighths of a mile "blow out." Secretariat powered through the stretch so impressively that those watching knew he had worked rapidly. Still, there were gasps when the *Daily Racing Form* clockers announced he had worked the three furlongs in :32 3/5, a half-mile in :44 4/5.

His picture and workout were headline news in the next day's *Form*, and the photo of him stretched out like a flying eagle made numerous newspapers around the nation. His coming-out party in the Bay Shore at nearby Aqueduct was certain to receive extraordinary attention.

The day of the race was gray and sometimes wet, producing a sloppy track on which Secretariat would face five other horses, among them Swift Stakes winner Champagne Charlie; Actuality, winner of the Hibiscus Stakes at Hialeah; and old juvenile rivals Impecunious and Torsion, the latter coming off a recent allowance race win at Aqueduct.

Almost 33,000 fans showed up, and almost all of them were on their feet for the seven-furlong Bay Shore, which started from the backstretch chute.

Secretariat, in post position four, got out of the gate well but half a furlong into the race was bumped solidly by Torsion, who had broken in the air and was struggling to get into stride. Secretariat wobbled briefly, then regained his stride and took off after the leaders.

As he picked up horses, Turcotte found himself stuck behind the leaders, with Champagne Charlie hemming him in on the rail. In early stretch, with Actuality and Impecunious in front of him and Champagne Charlie on their outside, it seemed plausible that Secretariat might lose due to poor positioning, but he would have none of it.

When a slight gap opened between Actuality and Impecunious, Secretariat barged through it like a full-back on the goal line. He burst clear and drew away to a four and a half-length win over Champagne Charlie. The final time for the Bay Shore's seven furlongs was 1:23 1/5, and Secretariat galloped out a mile in 1:37 4/5.

There was a disallowed claim of foul by jockey James Moseley on Impecunious, who got the worst of it when Secretariat set his sight on winning.

Much has been made of Dr. Manuel "Manny" Gilman's measurements of Secretariat just before the Bay Shore. Gilman, chief veterinarian for the New York Racing Association, routinely measured promi-nent horses for posterity, and his March 1973 version of Secretariat showed the colt to be 16.2 hands tall, possessed of a 75 1/5 inch girth, and weighing 1,160 pounds. According to a Charlie Hatton column, this made him taller, rounder, and heavier than Man o' War and Gallant Fox, two remarkable specimens.

Between the Bay Shore and his next start, the Gotham Stakes on April 7, Secretariat threw in some fast works, one of them a mile in 1:35 2/5 on March 28 (he galloped out a mile and one-eighth in 1:48 4/5), but his final serious work, on the Tuesday before the Gotham, was a five-furlong trip in 1:02 3/5 in the slop. Laurin wasn't thrilled with the effort, but it didn't stop Hall of Fame trainer Syl Veitch from saying, a few days later, to *The Blood-Horse*'s Ed Bowen, "Secretariat can run fast and far. I think he'll go down in history as another Man o' War."

Secretariat was facing five opponents in the one-mile Gotham, a one-turn affair starting from the backstretch chute, and only Champagne Charlie seemed to have a chance to trouble him.

Noting the lack of early speed in the field, Laurin and Turcotte considered asking Secretariat to use his great speed early in the race unless somebody went out faster than expected. Their thinking was long term: in the bigger races ahead, he might be tested by slow paces and better horses, so a more versatile running style could prove useful.

A large crowd of 41,998 turned out for the Gotham on a cool April day. They were surprised to see Secretariat move to the leaders down the backside, then take the lead after a half-mile, which was run in :45 1/5. Turcotte had him two lengths in front of Champagne Charlie as they turned for home, six furlongs in a rapid 1:08 3/5.

Then, for about a sixteenth of a mile, Champagne Charlie gradually gained ground on Secretariat, getting within a neck of him at the eighth pole. Secretariat, with two taps of the whip from his rider, found another gear and edged away from Charlie's challenge. He drew out to a three-length win in 1:33 2/5, equaling the track record.

Champagne Charlie had given the crowd, who bet Secretariat down to 1-10, an uncomfortable thrill, although it was noted that the winner had conceded nine pounds to the runner-up (126 to 117).

The Wood Memorial on April 21, two weeks prior to the Kentucky Derby, was going to be not only Secretariat's first racing trip over a mile and one-eighth, but also his launch for the Kentucky Derby and subsequent Triple Crown races.

The competition looked tougher, with Champagne Charlie back for more and Secretariat's stablemate Angle Light coming off sharp workouts. Step Nicely was also running, as well as a tall, handsome bay colt named Sham. By the top-class handicapper Pretense out of the Princequillo mare Sequoia, Sham was a Claiborne-bred. Had Bull Hancock not fallen terminally ill, Sham would almost certainly have been running in Claiborne's orange silks in the spring of 1973.

Instead, he had been sold to Sigmund Sommer, a leading New York owner, for $200,000 at Claiborne's dispersal in November 1972. Frank "Pancho" Martin, a native of Cuba with a thick Spanish accent and a marvelous eye for racing talent, became the colt's trainer. Pancho Martin was a superb horseman who loved to compete. The game, for him, was "my horse against your horse," and in Sham he felt he had a loaded gun, the best horse he'd ever trained.

Sham had made Martin even more confident with five wins at Santa Anita, the last coming in the nine-furlong Santa Anita Derby, where he handily beat Linda's Chief, although the latter colt was hampered badly early in the race by Sham's entry mate, Knightly Dawn.

Shipped from California to New York, Sham worked brilliantly for the Wood, including a five-eighths outing in :58 four days before the race.

Secretariat, meanwhile, had not worked particularly well after the Gotham, partly because Laurin eased
up on him following the fast time in the race. On the
day Sham did his :58, Secretariat went a mile in a slow
1:42 2/5, with Turcotte keeping him wrapped up
because of a loose horse on the track.

The slow workout concerned both Laurin and
Turcotte, but the stablehands who took care of
Secretariat were even more bothered by the colt's
apparent listlessness. Groom Eddie Sweat and exercise
rider Charlie Davis thought the big red colt simply was-
n't himself, and they weren't sure why.

Racing fans, knowing none of this, were focused on
a controversy inflamed by Charlie Hatton.

Hatton questioned Angle Light's credentials for the
race and also wondered if Pancho Martin's goal was to
gang up on Secretariat. Martin had put in both Sham
and Knightly Dawn, plus another Sommer colt,
Beautiful Music, the latter two apparently entered to
assure an earnest pace. Hatton wore his feelings about
these entries on his sleeve. Martin and Edwin
Whittaker, the owner of Angle Light, likewise exer-
cised their right to free speech after Hatton's first hints

of conspiracy, only to become more incensed when Hatton wrote the day before the Wood, "We shall not be surprised if the Tote board lights up with foul claims like Times Square on Saturday night. Our best advice is to hold all mutual tickets."

When Hatton invoked the names of the stewards as "insurance that nobody is going to prolong the race," a livid Martin scratched both Knightly Dawn and Beautiful Music, and told the press he blamed Laurin for Hatton's comments.

Meanwhile, Laurin's father-in-law died the week of the Wood, and Secretariat was not given the short, sharp pipe-opener he might have needed a couple of days before the race. Then, on the morning of the Wood, as Manny Gilman did his pre-race inspection and identification checks, he noticed a small abscess under Secretariat's upper lip. He showed it to Laurin, but told him he didn't think it would bother the colt.

Eddie Sweat, though, had problems getting Secretariat to accept the bit when he put the bridle on him prior to going to the paddock. Sweat thought the colt was uncomfortable, and so was the groom.

With Knightly Dawn and Beautiful Music out of the

race, the only speed in the Wood was Angle Light, and jockey Jacinto Vasquez sent the son of 1964 Belmont Stakes winner Quadrangle right to the lead, with Sham parked just behind them, although neither was in a hurry. Angle Light was cruising through tepid early fractions: :24 3/5 for the first quarter, :48 1/5 for a half, 1:12 1/5 after six furlongs.

He had a one and a half-length lead over Sham at that point, and the Sommer colt seemed poised to sweep by Angle Light at his leisure. Secretariat had reverted to his traditional style, dropping back early and staying outside into the final turn. Here, the red colt was supposed to pick up the pace on his own and then find his path to the leaders and blow by everyone, irrespective of the slow pace in front of him.

Later, Turcotte said his mount never seemed to push against the bit, nor did he begin leveling off as he always did for that relentless, never-hesitant rush to the finish line. Instead, Secretariat, drifting a bit in the stretch, never got into the race. He finished third, four lengths behind Angle Light and Sham, who were a head apart, in that order.

Secretariat's race, especially considering the slow

pace and his lack of a forward position early, would have been considered respectable had he been virtually any other horse.

Derby favorites — no, Triple Crown favorites — should be able to do better than that, particularly "superhorses." The crowd of 43,614 was stunned, except for the perpetual New York boo birds, who let Secretariat and Turcotte hear their views when the horse came back to be unsaddled.

Mostly, though, there was silence born of shock. Nowhere was the surprise and disappointment more profound than among the shareholders in the world's most expensive stallion prospect. Seth Hancock left quickly as the race ended, dismayed but subdued.

Penny Tweedy was anything but subdued. She was upset with Ed Whittaker for running Angle Light, although she was gracious to him after the race. She was upset with Laurin for allowing Angle Light to run and with Turcotte for not being more aware of the pace. She, of course, could not escape the burden of deciding the racing future of the sport's first six-million-dollar horse. A failure in the Derby would force her to think the unthinkable: Secretariat's retirement.

If there had been pressure on the Meadow Stable team before the Wood, it was multiplied immeasurably by Secretariat's flop at Aqueduct. The naysayers were now back and louder than ever:

Secretariat had hit the Bold Ruler "wall."

He was moody, like his sire, and raced up to his ability only when things went his way.

He was just a sprinter-miler who lost his punch when sent around two turns.

He had been "cooked" by all those fast workouts and races.

He was sore.

He had knee problems, hip problems, hock problems, arthritis, rheumatism, a recurrence of splints.

He was one-dimensional, had to have a lot of speed in front of him.

Rumors give racetrackers something to do with their "down" time, but the swell of negativism surrounding Secretariat after the Wood Memorial was almost unprecedented. The "superhorse" of April 20 became the "superflop" of April 21. Rarely had so many jumped ship so quickly, especially in Kentucky's breeding community where $190,000 per share was suddenly looking very rich.

To be fair, there was reason to question the Wood result. There was no way to make sense of it, unless fans bought into the notion that the lip abscess was the villain, and that was too simple or too suspect for the cynics. Secretariat had run a clunker, and all that could be done was to move on, put the colt back on the track, and hope the Wood had been an anomaly.

Surrounded by misgivings and second-guessing, the big youngster, looking as good as ever, was flown to Louisville, Kentucky, the Monday after the Wood. He was placed in stall 21 of barn 42, the same stall occupied by Riva Ridge prior to his 1972 Derby win.

Turcotte came to town for an April 27 workout, during which he and Vasquez sent Secretariat and Angle Light, respectively, six furlongs as a pair in 1:12 3/5. Turcotte still didn't think the horse was on his "A" game; he wasn't dropping down into the bit. Told about the abscess after his return to New York, Turcotte was immediately certain that that explained the Wood result.

The following Monday, April 30, Sham blew through a five-furlong workout in :59, pulling up after six furlongs in 1:11 1/5, further emboldening his fiery trainer, who was still angry over the brouhaha surrounding the

Wood Memorial. His colt was training beautifully and appeared to be blossoming physically, but a few observers noted that he had had every opportunity to run by Angle Light in the Wood and failed to do so.

Martin, meanwhile, seemed more consumed with beating Secretariat — and Laurin — rather than winning the Derby. His bravado aside, Pancho had a classy colt. Sham appeared to love the Churchill surface, which not every horse does, and was almost certain to handle the Derby trip.

Turcotte was back in Louisville for another workout on Wednesday, May 5, a five-furlong trip that was closely watched. This time, the Canadian-born rider felt what he was hoping to feel. Secretariat settled into stride and then picked up momentum steadily, finishing with power and enthusiasm. He was timed in :58 3/5, galloping out six furlongs in 1:12. Turcotte knew the best horse he'd ever ridden was right where he needed to be. The abscess was now history, and Secretariat was ready to make history.

CHAPTER 7

Roses And Records

T he Kentucky Derby has not, for a long time, simply been an important horse race. It is an event, something every horse fan has to experience at least once to pass from this earth peacefully.

Churchill Downs' management, mindful of the symbolism of the first Saturday in May, has carefully cultivated the image of the Derby as a world-class media event. It's a gathering of the who's who and wannabes of Thoroughbred racing, a social occasion of many parts, and — above all — a shrine, the true meaning of which can only be understood by those whose horse enters the winner's circle following the "most exciting two minutes in sports."

The Kentucky Derby is certainly the most sought-after race in the world and, as the first leg of the American Triple Crown, the start of horse racing's five weeks in the sun each spring. If the Derby were the second or third leg in the Triple Crown or held somewhere other than Kentucky, it might not have the same panache.

The ninety-ninth Kentucky Derby, run on May 5, 1973, carried a little extra glamour, precisely because racing people had been telling themselves that Meadow Stable possessed a panacea for what ailed the sport. The remedy came in the form of the flame-colored colt who set hearts aflutter and caused Pancho Martin to see red.

The consternation over Secretariat's performance in the Wood Memorial had, if anything, stirred more interest in the Derby, for now an element of mystery that had not existed before the Wood surrounded Secretariat .

Even his most ardent fans understood that any race-horse is beatable, but Secretariat's Wood was incomprehensible to virtually everyone in the sport. Fans wanted to throw it out, but they couldn't. They wanted to find an excuse for the horse, but they couldn't. Few people knew about the lip abscess, and it wouldn't have been given much credence had it been public record, as plausible as it was to Turcotte.

The Wood result impacted a lot of things, but nothing more important than the Derby's field size. When entries were drawn, a dozen horses lined up to face Secretariat, including a number of new faces.

Angle Light was there, following some Derby week sparring between Ed Whittaker and Penny Tweedy, who was still upset by the Wood loss and blamed several people, including Whittaker, for her horse's disaster in New York. She eventually apologized to Whittaker and wished him well in the Derby, but the tension remained.

Sham drew post-position four, and much media support was swinging his way, even though Pancho's barbs aimed at the Secretariat camp and his breezy confidence in his own horse were getting on people's nerves.

There were others deserving attention, such as the tough Our Native, winner of the Flamingo Stakes; Florida Derby winner Royal and Regal, who had a hoof bothering him; Shecky Greene, a brilliant sprinter and the likely Derby pacemaker; Blue Grass Stakes winner My Gallant, who was sure to stay the trip; and Forego, a giant gelding with intriguing potential but not much experience. He would eventually become a racing icon, but not yet.

The weather for Derby Day was perfect, with unblemished blue skies and a high of seventy degrees. The crowd, as it always does for the Derby, started to arrive early, eventually swelling Churchill Downs with 134,476 souls, at the time a record for the event.

The Meadow entourage was outwardly happy and confident but inwardly still reeling from the Wood and, perhaps, from the ugliness surrounding the entry situation in New York and the subsequent discomfort between Penny Tweedy and Ed Whittaker. Only Ron Turcotte seemed confident, believing that Secretariat was his old self and that if he let the horse run his race, Turcotte would win the roses for the second straight year.

Derby Day can seem like weeks to those with runners in the race, but the preliminaries were over and the horses were parading on the track to the tune of "My Old Kentucky Home," then warming up before being loaded in the gate. The vast Derby crowd, many hoping for a Secretariat victory, nonetheless hedged their bets, making the big horse and Angle Light 1.50-1 favorites as an entry, with Sham at 2.5-1.

Elmendorf Farm's Twice a Prince reared in the gate, briefly catching his legs on the front door. Once he was untangled, the load was finally completed. Secretariat was in post-position ten, so he was still outside the gate when Twice a Prince, in post-position six, acted up, giving Secretariat a possible advantage over those already in the gate, including Sham in post-position four.

It was post time. From the starting gate, thirteen three-year-olds looked out on the long Churchill Downs homestretch ready to make that first, intimidating run past the grandstand.

The first turn in the Derby is a relatively long haul from the gate, far enough to alleviate, to some extent, the crowding associated with what is, invariably, a large field.

Secretariat's first trip through "Derby Lane" was typical. The *Racing Form* chart caller said it perfectly: "Secretariat relaxed nicely and dropped back last leaving the gate as the field broke in good order..."

In post-race hindsight that comment was a good omen, but to the Meadow Stable onlookers, and

Secretariat's many fans, the colt's run down the front side was anything but encouraging.

Recalling most vividly his desultory Wood Memorial performance, they were collectively wringing their hands, forgetting that he had done much the same thing in ten of eleven starts prior to the Wood and had finished in front in all but one.

The Wood had been his first failure of style, and one could almost sense the "here we go again" feeling sweep over the crowd, including the horsemen in the box seats and dining areas at Churchill.

Turcotte, on the other hand, was as happy as the proverbial clam. His mount was safely away from any possible trouble at the start. Secretariat had eased over to the inside and was bowling along in a relaxed but eager state. He was running against the bit, unlike his race in the Wood and some of his post-Wood workouts, but not struggling with Turcotte. This was the Secretariat that the jockey knew and trusted.

Up front the lead belonged, as expected, to Shecky Greene, who had daylight between him and Gold Bag (who had made Secretariat look pedestrian in spring workouts when they were two-year-olds), with Royal and Regal third just ahead of Angle Light, with Sham and jockey Laffit Pincay Jr. beautifully positioned in fifth, less than three lengths off the lead.

Pincay was riding his textbook race, just what Pancho Martin had ordered. He was positioned toward the front, out of traffic and trouble, ready to pounce when asked. Many observers thought, at this point, it was Sham's race to lose. The mahogany colt had smashed his mouth on the side of the gate at the start and then bumped into Navajo before Pincay got him settled and into his best stride. Regardless, as they swept into the clubhouse turn, Sham — with two loose teeth — was traveling ominously well.

Secretariat had improved his position somewhat — from last to eleventh — after the opening quarter-mile, which was run in a solid :23 2/5. As the field moved through the first turn, he steadily began to pick up his pace.

There was no mad rush to the lead, no sudden surge that would propel him by the laggards, but instead a momentum-building drive that inexorably ate away at the leader's margin. "Shecky" had a three-length lead after a half-mile, run in :47 2/5, having slowed the pace in the second quarter, with Sham third behind Gold Bag, and Secretariat striding smoothly and purposefully along in sixth position, seven lengths off the pace.

At the pivotal half-mile pole, with six furlongs run in a moderate 1:11 4/5, Shecky Greene still had the lead by a length and a half, but Sham was sitting in second, perfectly placed for Pincay's call, which came midway around the turn.

The half-mile marker is often where the real battle for the Derby begins. Fearing traffic ahead, jockeys tend to send their mounts into the fray, hoping to get a position that will give them a clear shot when they turn into the stretch. The result, more often than not, is a free-for-all that creates the traffic jams the riders hoped to avoid. Horses are often used up prematurely, leaving the race to the few that still have the legs and the good fortune to have an open path.

In the 1973 Derby, however, the final turn was a scene of relative calm, for Sham was merely waiting for Pincay to push the button, with Shecky Greene and the lead in the ninety-ninth Kentucky Derby at his mercy.

Pincay urged Sham past Shecky Greene, without

pressure, while behind him there seemed to be little threat. At the mid-point of the turn, only one horse was moving faster than Sham.

Secretariat's resolute drive never faltered down the Churchill backside; indeed, it gained intensity as he strode by horses. As Sham made the final bend, the blue-and-white checked blinkers of Meadow Stable suddenly appeared in Pincay's peripheral vision.

The huge Derby crowd now sensed what was happening. Sham was doing what Pancho Martin had predicted, running the race of his life, a quarter of a mile from everlasting fame. Just off his left flank, the Meadow monster was in full flight, setting the stage for the stretch duel everyone had hoped to see.

The crowd's roar as the two horses turned for home was ear splitting, and Sham, feeling Pincay's whip, dug in to defend his lead. Secretariat, after drifting slightly on the turn, was forcing the issue relentlessly, with Turcotte at work with his stick.

For one hundred yards or so they were a team, and bedlam coursed from the crowd. A furlong out, it was clear that Secretariat had the better of it, his stride still strong, his action smooth and rhythmical. Gradually, he put daylight between himself and Sham, with Turcotte only showing him the whip to keep him focused.

Secretariat was in charge of this Derby, going away at the wire by two and a half lengths, with the tired but willing Sham eight lengths in front of third-place Our Native.

The riveting power of the stretch drive had so totally absorbed the crowd that it took a few moments for horsemen and fans to notice the timer display on the tote board: 1:59 2/5! It was a new Derby and track record, the first Derby ever run under two minutes. Northern Dancer's mark had been broken by three-fifths of a second.

The crowd realized history had been made and roared its approval and appreciation for an astounding performance as Secretariat and Turcotte made their way back to the winner's circle in Churchill's infield.

The emotions were many — relief and joy for Tweedy and Laurin, vindication for Turcotte and for the deceased Bold Ruler, a double thrill for Seth Hancock, watching his pressure-packed syndication effort pay off while the Claiborne-bred Sham ran the best Derby ever by a runner-up.

The second-guessing, including that of the colt's inner circle, was over, the naysayers put in their place. Secretariat had always seemed to be a rare specimen of an elite breed, a horse of incredible ability and scope, and in the right place at the right moment he had lived up to all the dreams, all the hype, all the expectations.

There had been no sudden rush around his field, no quick burst of speed at the opportune moment, no nimble move between horses at a critical juncture. Instead, Secretariat had, after warming to the task, simply ground up his field and tossed it aside.

An analysis of the fractional times and the race chart revealed a performance even more astounding than imagined. Secretariat's quarter-mile splits were as follows: :25 1/5, :24, :23 4/5, :23 2/5, and :23.

He had run each successive quarter faster than the previous one, the last half-mile in :46 2/5, the last six furlongs in 1:10 1/5, the last mile in 1:35 1/5. His final quarter was the fastest in Derby history by three-fifths of a second. These numbers were so amazing that one wondered if they could be accurate. Horses simply couldn't do that, could they? Only one had.

The crushing pressure on Penny Tweedy, Lucien Laurin, and Seth Hancock had been lifted. The six-million-dollar horse had done his job so spectacularly that $190,000 per share seemed quite reasonable, perhaps cheap. The numbness and stress that followed the Wood were now bad memories, and the Preakness was something to look forward to, another link in a chain of greatness. Secretariat and friends could travel to Baltimore with confidence and purpose.

The Preakness is the shortest of the Triple Crown events, a sixteenth of a mile shorter than the Derby, five sixteenths shorter than the Belmont. It is hardly a sprint, however, and its winners often come from off the pace, belying the race's reputation as speed favoring.

Pimlico Race Course, home to the Preakness, is one of America's oldest tracks, opened in 1870 on the outskirts of Baltimore. The city grew around the track, and now inner-city neighborhoods surround it on two sides and an upper-middle-class enclave on another.

The track itself is, like Churchill Downs, a mile in circumference, but jockeys and trainers believe it has tighter turns than Churchill, thus requiring aggressive, alert riding tactics and good tactical speed.

There is little empirical evidence to support this notion, but horsemen and riders swear by it and ride the track accordingly.

The Preakness, then, is all about tactical speed, one person's horse versus someone else's. It is a fallacy that horses have to be well positioned before the final turn at Pimlico and in striking position before the head of the stretch to win the Preakness. The facts are irrelevant; anecdotal evidence is all that is needed.

Secretariat, by all appearances, was a stronger, fitter horse after the Derby than beforehand. Veteran horsemen were hailing him as equal to Citation, Count Fleet, possibly even the great American legend Man o' War.

Sham, too, sore gums aside, had come out of the Derby in good shape, and he and Secretariat were shipped early to Baltimore, stabled in Barn EE, where all the Preakness horses stay, nine stalls apart: Secretariat in stall 41, Sham in 32.

Pancho Martin, still believing he had the better horse, was personally looking after Sham, although his rhetoric had cooled considerably after the heat of the Wood Memorial and the high-tension of Derby week. Sham had had things his way in Louisville, but that banged-up mouth at the start of the Derby might have been enough to tip the scales against the colt.

On Sunday morning, May 13, the rivals made their way to the Pimlico main track for serious five-furlong blowouts.

Sham was brilliant, ripping off his five-eighths in :58 2/5, a signal that he fully retained the verve he had shown at Churchill Downs.

Secretariat, with Turcotte aboard, made Sham look like a station wagon in a Formula One race. He sailed the half-mile in :45 1/5, nailed the five-eighths in :57 2/5, and galloped out six furlongs in 1:10. The doubts about him prior to the Derby were like chaff in the wind. Secretariat was breathtaking.

If the Preakness looked like a match race to racing writers and fans across America, it looked even more so to horsemen. Pimlico racing secretary Larry Abbundi's challenge was to find enough entrants to run for the minor prizes.

Of the other Derby starters, only Our Native was making the trip to Baltimore, so Abbundi started scratching around for a few others. He found a speed horse named Ecole Etage in a local barn, that of leading Maryland trainer Bud Delp, and talked trainer John Campo into sending Buckland Farm's Torsion, another speed type, from New York. Deadly Dream, winner of an allowance race over older horses at Penn National, was also entered, along with another local horse, The Lark Twist, who was later scratched.

Preakness Day on May 19 was gorgeous, a perfect mid-May day, and the lure of Secretariat, and his budding rivalry with Sham, encouraged 61,657 to Pimlico, exceeding the previous record by twenty-one percent.

For the Meadow Stable entourage, the hours leading up to the Preakness would provide unexpected adventure that must have made them wonder if this was not to be their day.

The Tweedys decided to have lunch at the Pimlico Hotel, which was noted for its crabcakes (like most Maryland restaurants) and was only a couple of blocks from the track's main entrance.

Lunch arrived along with the news a valet had damaged several cars including theirs in a parking mishap.

Upon arrival at the clubhouse entrance, they discovered there were no credentials in their name, so they broke with racing tradition and paid their way into the track, comforted in knowing that at least they would get their money's worth by watching their hero in action.

The Preakness horses are always saddled on the track's turf course, just below the finish line, a tradition which allows thousands of people to see the horses and their human connections in the moments before battle. For the Tweedys, the saddling experience had some added, unwelcome, touches. Penny Tweedy had her arm burned by a cigarette while on the turf course, then her husband, John, on his way to the trackside box seats, had his wallet filched by a local entrepreneur. Finally in their seats, they waited anxiously to see how the race would unfold tactically, specifically, what Sham would do.

Pancho Martin decided that his colt might have been sent after Shecky Greene a bit too soon in the Derby, so in the paddock, he told Pincay to get a good position, sit a few lengths off the pace, then go to the leaders only when they began to back up. Thinking Sham only needed a bit more juice to handle Secretariat's late rush, Martin wanted Pincay to keep some fuel in the horse's tank.

The post parade and start for the ninety-eighth Preakness were uneventful, with Secretariat, favored at .30-1, breaking smoothly and easing back as Turcotte let the red colt find his stride and get into the race. Sham broke at a right angle, bumped slightly with Deadly Dream, then set off in pursuit of Ecole Etage and Torsion, who were already leading the small field.

Ecole Etage, in fact, got an easy jump heading into the first turn, reaching the first quarter teletimer in :25, a pedestrian clocking, with Torsion and Sham tracking him. Surprisingly, Secretariat was fourth, five and a half lengths back of Ecole Etage and already beginning to move forward. Perhaps the slowness of the pace had, inadvertently, left him closer to the lead than usual, or perhaps something else was happening.

The "something else" was soon evident. Turcotte, loving the smooth, eager power he was feeling under him, sensed the pace was slow and might get slower as George Cusimano on Ecole Etage, under no pressure, tried to relax his horse and steal the race.

Turcotte asked Secretariat to take hold of the bit, and when he did, the response was startling. With his ground-eating twenty-five-foot stride fully engaged,

Secretariat, ignoring the law of physics that says an object moves faster on a straight path, swept by the horses in front of him in the first turn and was on the lead as the field turned down the backstretch.

Onlookers were stunned, none more so than Lucien Laurin, who thought his jockey had lost his mind and the Preakness.

Turcotte, however, not only knew what he was doing but also understood better than anyone else the almost unfathomable energy under his saddle. Secretariat was galloping along majestically, totally in control of himself and his race.

The official time for the second quarter was :23 4/5, which meant Secretariat had run :22 and change on the turn, an amazing dash for a big-framed, hulking horse around a turn on a mile track.

Secretariat was up by a half-length after a half-mile (officially :48 4/5) and had widened his lead to two and a half lengths by the time he reached the half-mile pole, officially timed in 1:12.

If the teletimer could be believed, Secretariat, all alone and running freely but comfortably, would have to fall down to lose. Pincay had fully engaged Sham.

He earnestly pursued his chestnut tormenter, but the best of Sham — which was very good — was likely ill-equipped for the Herculean task before him.

Secretariat led Sham by two and a half lengths when the pair reached the stretch (officially in 1:36 1/5). Secretariat charged confidently along, with Turcotte hand riding him. Sham was under pressure from Pincay and responding vigorously, but he simply couldn't cut into that two and a half-length lead. One had the sense that Sham was as deep into his reserves as he could get, while Secretariat, treating his rival almost contemptuously, had an additional gear, or two, on hold. He was on overdrive, saving fuel, while his competition was running on fumes.

They passed the finish as they had in the Derby, Secretariat winning by two and a half relaxed lengths, Sham second by eight over Our Native, who had a length on Ecole Etage. The final time was a good 1:55, a clocking that had only been exceeded twice in the prior history of the Preakness, but a bit disappointing to many who believed Secretariat was on a record-shattering mission to glory.

While the Woodlawn Vase was being presented and

champagne toasts were being hoisted, all hell was breaking loose among the press.

Daily Racing Form clockers Gene "Frenchy" Schwartz and Frank Robinson reported to *Form* columnist Joe Hirsch that while working in separate locations, they had each hand-timed Secretariat in 1:53 2/5, a radical difference from the teletimer number.

Hirsch reported that information to Pimlico officials and wrote about it in his report of the race. Other writers, many of them great admirers of Secretariat, also picked up the story and started insisting on a review of the proceedings.

Pimlico management, meanwhile, concluded that the teletimer had malfunctioned, likely from the start (it had probably started belatedly), causing Ecole Etage's first quarter time (:25) to be incorrect (too slow), with the resulting fractions all similarly affected.

A racing official, usually the paddock judge, routinely times each race by hand as a backup in the event of a teletimer failure or malfunction. The Pimlico official responsible for having his stopwatch on during the 1973 Preakness was E.T. McLean, who, when asked, said he caught Secretariat in 1:54 2/5.

CBS, which televised the Triple Crown races at the time, weighed in with evidence from the timing of its videotape of the race and from comparing Secretariat's race tape time with that of Canonero II, who had set the Preakness record in 1971 with a final time of 1:54.

Finally, the Maryland Racing Commission, trying to calm the insistent reporters and restless fan inquiries, held a hearing at which virtually everybody who wanted to speak did so. They listened to the teletimer story, the *Racing Form* clockers' story, McLean's story, and the CBS story.

Concluding they had no firm basis for accepting any single account, they decreed that McLean's 1:54 2/5 stopwatch time would be official.

That was that, and still is. The *Racing Form* chart of the race carries, and always will, a note that says, in parentheses, "*Daily Racing Form* Time 1:53 2/5 New Track Record." The official fractions were revised to :24 2/5, :48 1/5, 1:11 2/5, 1:35 3/5, and 1:54 2/5.

Horsemen are fond of saying that race times, like time in prison, are irrelevant. In this case, though, time really meant something, especially to those who fervently believed Secretariat had set a Preakness record to go with his new Derby standard.

In a few weeks, the controversy would mean even more.

CHAPTER 8

A Tremendous Machine

K ent Hollingsworth, racing writer, raconteur, and editor of *The Blood-Horse*, was known for his skepticism and parsimonious use of laudatory phrases when describing class in racehorses. However, in his opinion column in the magazine's May 28, 1973, edition, Hollingsworth could not contain his enthusiasm.

"Up close, bigness is overwhelming...

"We just saw Secretariat come from last place in the Preakness, go three horses wide on the first turn, take command at the six-furlong pole, ignore the futile challenge of a good horse, and coast home without the boy even turning his whip.

"This close, the bigness is awesome.

"In his one race here, what more could Phar Lap have done to impress veteran horsemen? What more could Ribot or Sea-Bird have done to impress European horsemen who saw them race but twice?

"There are wise Turfman, standing fast with treasured recollections of Citation and Equipoise, and Twenty Grand, and Exterminator, who wait for Secretariat to win the Belmont and Triple Crown, to carry the weight of Discovery against an older generation, to race uphill and down around the sweeping turn at Longchamp, before declaring greatness here.

"There is something very special about this big, free-running colt, something so apparent it requires not the practiced eye of the horsemen. It was seen by a record crowd at the Kentucky Derby, and it lured a record crowd to the Preakness, a crowd whose enthusiasm broke through security lines and caused a rush to the infield rail to cheer on this exceptional colt through his powerful stretch run.

"And as Secretariat galloped along in the shadow of the Pimlico stands, emerging suddenly in the gloriously bright sun of the finish line, we stood there, awed, and then joined the applause which had accompanied his run for the last eighth-mile.

"If this were not the performance of a great horse, we have not seen one."

Preakness record or no Preakness record, Secretariat's superior performances in the first two Triple Crown races had enraptured Turf writers and commentators one and all and had kindled an interest in horse racing not present since the time of Native Dancer.

The career of "the Dancer" had coincided with the early days of mass-market network television, a time when generations of Americans sat huddled in front of small screens with black-and-white, sometimes indistinct, images.

Native Dancer was a large, long-striding gray, a perfect contrast in the black-and-white world of television in the early fifties. His powerful closing rush added drama to his races, making him even more appealing. He was racing's first — and until the spring of 1973, biggest — television star.

Secretariat was returning to his home track, Belmont Park, as racing's biggest hero since — well, you pick the horse. From a media standpoint it would be Native Dancer. Horsemen, though, were reaching further back, to Citation, Count Fleet, even Man o' War. Contemporary trainers, even those longest of tooth, rarely had personal recall of the red-coated son of Fair

Play who became a dominant sports figure of the post-World War I era; nevertheless, Man o' War was America's most fabled Thoroughbred, the standard to which all before or after him would be compared.

Of all the great and near-great racehorses since Man o' War, only Citation had been consistently accorded similar status. His remarkable three-year-old season, in which he won nineteen of twenty starts, is thought of as perhaps the finest individual year ever among American Thoroughbreds.

Whereas Man o' War combined remarkable power and cat-like athleticism in one specimen, Citation was more workmanlike, a grind-it-out sort who would not be denied. They were fire and ice, but they were the benchmarks for succeeding generations.

Secretariat possessed qualities of each, a massive physical presence with the color and markings of a show horse. He didn't have Man o' War's tear-away manner, but he ran with a mind of his own. Secretariat's grinding style in the Derby and Preakness was reminiscent of Citation's.

Secretariat's handsome looks, and those spectacular sub-two-minute bursts at Churchill Downs and

Pimlico, made him a target for every newsperson and photographer who could find his or her way to Belmont, and lots of them did.

Secretariat had captured the nation's imagination, something editors and network executives quickly recognized. For the first time in the era of high-speed communications, a racehorse was a genuine star, a glamorous figure getting attention usually reserved for the biggest human sports personalities of the moment.

The week after the Preakness, Secretariat was the cover boy for *Newsweek*, *Time*, and *Sports Illustrated*, the first horse ever to make all three covers. *Time* and *Newsweek* both labeled him "Superhorse." Secretariat had returned racing to the front pages and was giving his sport its fifteen minutes in the sun, momentarily setting aside the years of media disinterest and missed opportunities.

Penny Tweedy, the most attractive, articulate, and thoughtful member of the Meadow team, was its natural spokesperson. She thrived on the intensity of the press coverage, including an appearance on NBC's "Today Show," in the days following the Preakness. Despite questions from reporters that were sometimes inane and often outlandish, she was always unfailingly charming, patient, and direct in her responses.

She retained the services of the William Morris Agency, the largest and best-known talent agency, to assist her with the public relations crush and advise her on the most effective ways to manage the demands for the use of Secretariat's image. He was suddenly the rage, a dazzlingly successful celebrity, unique in his appeal as an accomplished athlete and a majestic physical presence. He had it all — looks, style, and charisma.

One thing he didn't have, at least not yet, was a Triple Crown. The Belmont was still ahead, its daunting mile and a half the downfall of many Triple Crown hopes and dreams.

Almost forgotten in the dazzle and hype was the widespread belief that sons and daughters of Bold Ruler, however fast and courageous, were not stayers. Those who had doubted Secretariat's distance capacity, especially after his embarrassment in the Wood Memorial, were now silent. Amazingly, the questions about the colt's stamina limitations seemed to disappear at a time when they should have been the only question remaining about him. It was as if the Belmont were being conceded to him, such had been the effect of his Derby and Preakness performances. So awed were people by his brilliance at Churchill Downs and Pimlico that they seemed willing to ignore completely the skepticism so rampant a few weeks before.

Lucien Laurin had trained horses for three decades, but he had never seen or been part of anything like this. The media scrutiny was intense and ceaseless. Secretariat's every move was recorded; there were stories about his eating and sleeping habits, his grooming schedule, even his moods.

Laurin was, however, as focused as he had ever been on a horse's training. He felt that he now knew what it took to get this particular horse fit and primed for his best effort, and it involved lots of work — long and vigorous gallops interspersed with workouts over race distances at racing speed.

The program Secretariat followed was remarkable, one that had trainers shaking their heads in amazement at both the demands being placed on the Meadow colt and his responses.

Eight days after the Preakness, Laurin sent Secretariat and Turcotte six furlongs in 1:12 1/5, a smooth, almost playful romp that was only maintenance for this incredible horse. Five days later, on June 1, Secretariat worked a mile in what was supposed to be the colt's ultimate screw-tightening, pre-Belmont move. Laurin was looking for a 1:36 or so time, which would have been sensational, attracting headlines in racing trade papers and sports sections across the country.

Instead, what Laurin — and a battalion of writers, photographers, television camera crews, horsemen, and curiosity seekers — witnessed was a morning spectacle, an exhibition of strength, speed, and youthful exuberance that had to be seen to be believed.

For those who watched Secretariat run that morning, it was hard to reconcile that this was the colt who only a year before had been hard pressed to stay close to horses by now forgotten and that this was the colt who had not been routinely expected to produce high-speed workouts.

From the moment Turcotte set him alight down Belmont's yawning backstretch, Secretariat was on fire. He dashed through the first quarter-mile in :23 4/5, the half in :47, five-eighths in :58 4/5, three-quarters in 1:11, and seven furlongs in 1:22 4/5. The mile that

Laurin wanted in 1:36 was completed in 1:34 4/5, with nine furlongs, galloping, done in 1:48 3/5.

Secretariat came back kicking and playing. He was a live wire on four legs, although Laurin was concerned that he might have overdone it. As awed as they were by the workout, other veteran observers, including many trainers and writers, privately believed, too, that it might have been too fast. Laurin's was the old-fashioned way of training horses; he had to find out what his horse was made of *before* he went into battle, not during the battle. Those kinds of workouts were referred to as "hanging 'em on the fence" and were something of a lost art in the more sensitive world of modern Thoroughbred racing. "Sunny Jim" Fitzsimmons would have approved of Laurin's tack, but few trainers had Mr. Fitz's practical confidence or decades of hard-won experience.

Secretariat would get one final eye-opener, a routine — for him — half-mile in :46 3/5 on Wednesday, June 6, three days before the biggest day of his life.

The almost unanimous belief that the cover boy had the Belmont at his mercy had its disbelievers, of course, among them Pancho Martin, who still thought

Sham had not yet been beaten in a fair fight. He thought Secretariat was vulnerable if Sham could get the jump on him early and dictate the pace. He felt Sham had been used too quickly in the Derby and had been surprised by Secretariat's sudden sprint past his field on the first turn at Pimlico. This time, there would be no surprises. Sham would come out running, and let the big red lug chase him.

On the face of it, Martin had a plausible argument. Sham had run terrific races in both Kentucky and Maryland, record-setting or near-record performances on their own. One could concede that he might have been closer in the Derby had he not played smash mouth with the starting gate. And in the Preakness, his sideways lurch out of the gate, followed by a bump, then a brush with the inside rail going into the first turn, was not helpful to his chances.

Still, Martin and a lot of people were missing one important point: in both the Derby and Preakness, Secretariat acted like a stayer, running more strongly in the final stages of the race than earlier. His Preakness was, in fact, a textbook example of how true classic horses often win their races: use tactical speed to seize control of the race before it reaches its critical phase, then gallop on strongly enough to rebuff all challenges.

In other words, Secretariat looked like the very thing most thought he would not be, based on his male line and his power-packed conformation: a resolute stayer with a high traveling rate. These are rare racehorses, the types who end up on magazine covers or in paintings and in halls of fame.

Was Secretariat about to become one of them, or was he already there?

The Belmont is the oldest American classic, dating to 1867, and the longest. It was founded with the notion that America needed a functional equivalent, on dirt, of the Derby Stakes at Epsom, for a couple of centuries the most prestigious race in the world for three-year-olds.

Arguably, until perhaps the 1930s, the Belmont was the most sought-after Triple Crown race, mostly because the major private breeders who dominated top-class American racing maintained their stables in New York, and to them, the Belmont's one and a half miles was the ultimate test of a classic three-year-old, the proving ground for champions.

The Derby eventually grabbed the glamour and associated prestige, and the Triple Crown as an event became meaningful enough that the Belmont became less individually relevant.

Changes in the commercial breeding industry, ironically driven by the success of American-breds in Europe, led to greater popularity for the high-class milers and middle-distance performers that are the core of American racing, and greater attention to the races in which they competed.

Hence, a three-year-old running a mile and a half in June, even in traditionally significant races, was not as important to owners and breeders as this sort of horse had been throughout much of the sport's history. The English Derby and the Belmont had long been considered leading incubators of superior stallions; that they no longer were considered such said much about the path of racing in the latter portion of the twentieth century.

The 105th Belmont Stakes, though, had about as much impact, imagery, expectation, and hope attached to it as could be packed into one race. Secretariat, had he been able to comprehend the things being written and said about him, would probably have been a nervous wreck, if only because the weight of the sports world was upon his powerful shoulders.

Standing between him and his anticipated ascension to equine immortality were — in addition to Sham — Twice a Prince, the stoutly bred Elmendorf Farm colt who had delayed the start of the Derby and had no pretensions to being in the same class as the top two; My Gallant, a flop in the Derby but a recent winner at Belmont; and Pvt. Smiles, a well-bred son of Claiborne sire Herbager. Pvt. Smiles' primary claim was that he was bred and owned by the august stable of C.V. Whitney. Pancho Martin talked about putting Knightly Dawn in with Sham, but only if the track were wet, a condition that did not happen.

It was a sunny but humid day as a crowd of 67,605 came to Belmont to see if one horse out of the 24,361 Thoroughbreds registered in 1970 could accomplish something not seen since 1948, the year Citation powered to his Triple Crown victory.

Secretariat, honed for a distance he had never been before, would break from post-position one, with Sham in number five, and Pvt. Smiles, My Gallant, and Twice a Prince in between, in that order. This was almost surely going to be a two-horse race, the main question being which of the two would take over the track first. In the paddock and during the post parade, Secretariat remained calm and dry while Sham was sweating heavily and seemed unusually edgy.

At 5:38 p.m., with almost unbearable tension surrounding them, the field for the 1973 Belmont was sent on its way.

It was unclear where the speed in the race might come from, and both Laurin and Turcotte were prepared to send Secretariat to the front if no one else wanted to set the pace.

Secretariat broke sharply, by his standards, getting away evenly with the other four and running with purpose from the outset. The others — apart from Sham — were content to settle in behind Secretariat as they made their way into the first turn.

Pincay, knowing Martin wanted Sham on the lead, sent him quickly alongside Secretariat with the intent of passing the favorite. Turcotte, wanting to keep the inside path secure, sent Secretariat along the rail, asking him to go with Sham, who was parked just outside him, being hustled along by Pincay.

Instead of settling into a steady, long-distance type of pace, the two accelerated, Secretariat turning things up a notch but running easily, Sham pressing harder.

They passed the first quarter-mile in :23 3/5, fast time for a twelve-furlong race. Surely, they would relax a bit in the second quarter, pull back on the throttle.

But, no, Pincay pushed Sham to a slight lead, a head, a neck, a half-length, and Secretariat went with him, inching back toward the front, running rhythmically alongside the driving Sham.

A half-mile in :46 1/5, the fastest in Belmont history! What were these jockeys doing? Had they lost all sense of pace, conscious only of each other?

By this time, Secretariat and Sham had seven lengths over My Gallant and Twice a Prince.

Secretariat started to edge away from Sham in the next furlong, hitting the five-eighths mark in :58 1/5. He powered his way along with awesome precision, rolling past six furlongs in 1:09 4/5, the fastest such clocking in race history by three-fifths of a second.

The crowd, especially the horsemen, was astounded. This was amazing, but surely the red colt couldn't last. Surely Turcotte would get him to relax a bit now that Sham was done, falling away steadily toward the back of the pack.

Turcotte knew only that his horse was running fast and that he was doing so on his own, relaxed and comfortable. With a half-mile to go, the duo was seven lengths in front and widening the margin with every stride, flying past the half-mile marker in 1:34 1/5 for the first mile, another Belmont Stakes first.

Incredible, amazing, unsustainable.

Or was it?

As Secretariat and Turcotte raced around the middle of the seemingly endless final turn, track announcer Chic Anderson, as stunned as anyone else by what was unfolding in front of him, captured the moment perfectly:

"Secretariat is widening now. He is moving like a tremendous machine!"

The Belmont was now a race between Secretariat and himself, with the others falling farther and farther back. He was running alone, for all practical purposes in the midst of a long, very fast workout.

Halfway through the turn he reached a mile and one-eighth in 1:46 1/5, equaling the existing world record for the distance, doing it all on his own, with Turcotte just sitting quietly aboard, conscious of doing nothing to interfere with his partner's sweeping, ground-consuming stride.

Turning for home, the grand chestnut was twenty lengths in front, and he had run one and a quarter miles in 1:59, a second faster than the track record, two-fifths of a second faster than his record final Derby time.

The result was no longer in doubt, only the magnitude of the performance. No one in the massive crowd had seen anything remotely resembling this race, and as Secretariat pounded through the final quarter-mile there would be no let-up.

Twenty-eight lengths in front at the eighth pole (one and three-eighths miles in 2:11 1/5, faster than Man o' War's world record for the distance), he was making history with every gigantic step.

Turcotte, able to see the teletimer now and surprised at the race fractions, pushed his mount to keep driving to the wire, reaching for a record.

And then came the finish line. Secretariat and Turcotte crossed in splendid isolation, to thunderous roars and applause. For Tweedy, Laurin, Seth Hancock, and the breeders who had paid $190,000 a share for Secretariat's breeding rights only a few months before, this was a moment of supreme elation. But what they had witnessed was so startling, so far beyond anything they had seen before or expected, that they were reduced to stares of amazement and meaningless platitudes. They were exhilarated yet virtually speechless, so incomprehensible was this outcome.

Spectators cheered wildly for the first Triple Crown winner in twenty-five years. They were cheering a startling thirty-one-length margin over Twice a Prince, who was second by a half-length over My Gallant. (Sham — as gallant and able as Thoroughbreds come — faded so badly that he was beaten more than forty-five lengths, a sad end to his courageous Triple Crown saga.)

They were cheering a final time of 2:24. Yes, 2:24, the fastest Belmont ever by 2 3/5 seconds, the fastest mile and a half ever on an American dirt track.

They were cheering the most incredible two and a half minutes in American racing history.

They were cheering a legend.

Secretariat was no longer a rarity among Thoroughbreds. He was singular.

CHAPTER 9

Superhorse

T he verdict on Secretariat and his Belmont in the days afterward was virtually unanimous: greatest racehorse ever, greatest performance ever.

Indeed, he seemed to be perfection on the hoof, a superbly crafted individual with a placid temperament, exceptional intelligence, remarkable soundness, and the ability to run as fast and as far as racehorses are asked to go in modern racing.

Trainers, jockeys, owners, and breeders were uniformly impressed with the colt, awed by his appearance and his talents. The veterans compared him favorably with the best horses they'd ever seen, and the newcomers made him their frame of reference in judging greatness.

So, what was next? What do you do with a horse that has just broken everything but the sound barrier in three consecutive races. Not only was Secretariat the ninth Triple Crown winner, he had set official time records in two of the three races, and everybody except the official clocker thought the son of Bold Ruler had set a record in the other.

Blood-Horse editor Kent Hollingsworth judged, reasonably, that the remaining major stakes on the Thoroughbred racing calendar in 1973 would not add to or detract from the horse's reputation or value, and he offered the notion that an exciting and fitting challenge could be found in France's Prix de l'Arc de Triomphe, the one-and-a-half-mile, weight-for-age race for three-year-olds and up in October that, more often than not, settles who is Europe's best horse.

The Arc idea was intriguing, although in June of his three-year-old season the only experience Secretariat had had with grass was eating it.

He was now, truly, America's horse, a celebrity discussed on the talk shows and written about by columnists who never broached horse racing; Secretariat was a national icon.

The offers poured in, along with the fan mail. Secretariat could have appeared anywhere, been on the cover of any publication, shown up at any racetrack, even if only for a paddock appearance. There were even whispers that he should be retired, since he surely could never equal or surpass his majestic Belmont performance.

Penny Tweedy had, publicly and privately, committed to race the colt through the summer and fall, assuming his health and his form were in good order. The thought was to bring him back at Saratoga, in the Jim Dandy Stakes for three-year-olds, or the Whitney Stakes, for three and up, followed by the Travers.

All being well, he would then march through the key fall stakes in New York — the Woodward and Jockey Club Gold Cup — with a possible grass race or two added to the schedule (provided Secretariat worked well on the surface), although nothing was set in stone.

A few days after the Belmont, officials from Arlington Park, in suburban Chicago, contacted Tweedy. Arlington wanted to stage a three-horse race involving Secretariat; the classy Linda's Chief, who had skipped the Triple Crown races because trainer Al Scotti, believing his horse to be a miler, did the right thing for his horse; and Our Native, a distant third in the Derby and Preakness.

Arlington offered $125,000 in prize money, and either a mile or a mile and one-eighth as the race distance. Scotti didn't want to run, and Laurin didn't want to bring Secretariat back to a mile, so the proposition looked shaky and might have fallen through had Arlington management not persevered, chasing everybody with a decent three-year-old and a phone number.

Oddly enough, Laurin and Tweedy were the ones most eager to run their horse. Secretariat was bursting with energy, even after the apparent rigors of his Belmont, and the Meadow team also wanted to give Midwestern fans a chance to see him.

Finally, Arlington was able to assemble a four-horse field, going a mile and one-eighth, with Secretariat facing Our Native, My Gallant, and Blue Chip Dan. The Triple Crown winner would carry 126 pounds, the others 120, and the other three horses would be coupled as a single entry for betting purposes.

Arlington management wasn't worried about the wagering on the so-called Arlington Invitational. They knew a box-office draw when they saw one.

The local media were all over the big horse, even before he arrived, and hundreds of people came to see exercise rider Charlie Davis gallop the colt one and a quarter miles the day before the race. Chicago Mayor Richard Daley declared Saturday, June 30, as Secretariat Day. The horse got a proclamation, a key to the city, and lots of friendly police attention. Daley's city, for a few days, became Secretariat's city.

Prior to leaving for Chicago, Turcotte worked Secretariat five furlongs in :58 1/5, galloping out six furlongs in 1:12, a signal that the colt still had his Triple Crown edge or something close enough to keep Laurin happy.

Arlington Park was a happening place on race day. The 41,223 attendees were notably young and laden with cameras. The crowd was a racetrack marketing executive's dream come true.

Secretariat did his part, and with enough style to please everybody.

There is no encore after climbing Mount Everest or winning the Belmont by thirty-one lengths, but Secretariat did his reputation no harm. He broke slowly and awkwardly but was straightened away by Turcotte while going three-wide into the clubhouse turn, establishing a clear and easy lead. He was relaxed, almost lackadaisical, as he traveled through the opening quarter-mile in :24 4/5 and the half in :48, leading second-place My Gallant by three lengths.

Running as he pleased, with Turcotte simply steering, Secretariat quickened the pace, reaching six furlongs in 1:11 1/5. He then started to ease away on the final turn, actually gaining momentum as he rounded the bend.

In the stretch he was all alone, to the appreciative cheers of the fans in the packed Arlington facility, clicking off the mile in 1:35 while staying in the middle of the track.

Turcotte let him ramble through the final furlong for a relaxed win, stopping the teletimer in 1:47, a fifth of a second off the track record, which would have been his for the taking had Secretariat been asked to extend himself more. Secretariat's final margin over My Gallant was nine lengths, with Our Native a neck farther back in third.

The crowd loved it, and Tweedy and Laurin were relieved. The colt had clearly suffered no ill effects from his moonshot in the Belmont, and his foray to the Midwest as a gift to his fans had worked out beautifully.

Next, it was back to Belmont Park, with Saratoga next on the victory tour. The ultimate Saratoga goal was the historic Travers Stakes, the "Midsummer Derby," but the thought was to give Secretariat a prep race in either the Whitney Handicap, in which he would face older horses and give them weight, or in the Jim Dandy Stakes for three-year-olds, in which he would also be making weight concessions.

One former rival would be at neither race. Sham was found to have a hairline fracture in one of his forelegs after a workout in early July. Surgery followed and there was talk about an eventual return to racing, but he was retired to stud instead, and a game and generous racehorse was no longer part of the show.

Meantime, Philip Morris marketing chief Jack Landry, a racing fan, had talked his fellow executives into sponsoring a new race at Belmont Park in the autumn. It would be named the Marlboro Cup, after the tobacco company's flagship brand, and would carry a $250,000 purse. Beyond that, it was a work in progress, but certainly Landry's goal was to involve Secretariat, whether against Linda's Chief in a match race or stablemate Riva Ridge or a combination thereof.

While Landry and the New York Racing Association were sorting the details, Laurin was keeping his stable ace in fighting trim for the Whitney or Jim Dandy. The colt worked six furlongs in a decent 1:13 3/5 on July 10, then came back at seven furlongs on a sloppy track six days later in 1:25.

Laurin seemed satisfied with those efforts, but Turcotte, privately, wasn't so sure, feeling that Secretariat was not quite right, that the usual sparkle, the steady drumbeat style that could click off twelve-second furlongs in unending sequence, was missing.

On July 27, eight days before the Whitney, the colt went a mile in 1:34 in the slop at Saratoga, faster than the track record for the distance.

That was more like it, or was it? On Wednesday, August 1, several thousand people came to Saratoga early to see Secretariat work a half-mile in :48 1/5, not the usual stem-winder Laurin liked to see just before a race, but perhaps a logical follow-up to the fast mile four days before.

The Whitney featured four other horses, all older, all with significant credentials in the handicap division. One of them, Onion, had set a track record at Saratoga on July 31, running six and a half furlongs in 1:15 1/5. Trained by Allen Jerkens, a man noted for taking modestly bred performers and knocking off the stars of the sport, Onion was a potential threat, as was the talented True Knight, who had won the 1972 Jerome and Roamer handicaps.

None of them would matter, obviously, if the big red colt ran his typical race.

Whitney Day was hot and humid, and the track was still drying out from the previous day's heavy rain. Although labeled fast, the track was deep enough that jockeys in earlier races were avoiding the rail.

Secretariat banged his head on the starting-gate door just before the start, never a good omen, then broke more slowly than usual, dropping back to fourth as the field headed into the first turn. Turcotte decided to save ground and slipped him to the inside rail. As they headed onto the backstretch, they started to pick up horses, though in a more workmanlike manner than usual.

Onion had taken the lead at the outset and was comfortably clear of the field going down the backside, setting moderate fractions (:24 2/5 for the first quarter, the half-mile in :47 4/5). Secretariat sat on the rail until the half-mile pole, at which point he started to move inside Onion.

This, however, was not Secretariat's standard move, his surging, relentless, got-you-by-the-throat rush that had won a Triple Crown. The colt dug in and tried, but it was evident in the final furlong that this was not going to be his day.

Onion held on grimly, actually increasing the slight advantage he had in mid-stretch after a mile in 1:36. When they strode under the wire, Onion held a length advantage, with Rule by Reason closing strongly to fin-ish only a half-length behind Secretariat in third place. The final time was an unexceptional 1:49 1/5.

The atmosphere at Saratoga was one of shock and gloom, the crowd not wanting to believe what it had seen. CBS television commentators emptily attempted to explain the result. Racing fans everywhere were stunned, even more so than after the Wood Memorial.

This couldn't be happening. The Superhorse had turned mortal, beaten by something called Onion. Hopefully, a plausible explanation was forthcoming.

The following day Secretariat was running a temperature, as he had off and on the week before, and his bowel movements were loose. Appearing to be the victim of a virus, he was treated with antibiotics and walked for a few days. Laurin said that although the colt continued to eat well, he was extremely listless in the days after the race.

Saratoga's reputation as the "graveyard of champions," a legacy that includes Man o' War and Gallant Fox among its victims, had claimed Secretariat, as well.

Looking forward was difficult because Secretariat's health, for the first time in his career, was questionable. The Travers was out, and the Marlboro Cup, a race built with him in mind, was highly questionable.

Absent a clear physical reason not to do so, Laurin continued training the colt, watching for indications as to his general fitness and well being and a sign of his normal verve.

For a few precious weeks, the signals were mixed. Secretariat worked five furlongs in 1:00 3/5 on August 30, a mediocre move, especially for a horse preparing to face the best Thoroughbreds in training on the North American continent in only sixteen days.

Seven furlongs in 1:24 2/5 on September 3 did not

impress Laurin, nor did a 1:37 mile four days later.

Riva Ridge, on the other hand, was working brilliantly for the race, turning in a dazzling :57 1/5 five furlongs on Tuesday, September 11. Tweedy, with a soft spot for Riva Ridge, thought he was back to his springtime form of the previous year and would beat Secretariat in the Marlboro.

Riva Ridge, had, in fact, recovered a good bit of his confidence and reputation since the beatings he had taken in the fall of 1972. He had captured three of his prior four starts, one of them a world-record-setting victory in the Brooklyn Handicap, in which he edged True Knight and Tentam, carrying 127 pounds to their 117 and 119, respectively, and racing a mile and three-sixteenths in 1:52 2/5. He was, both Laurin and Tweedy believed, primed for a huge effort.

He would have to be, because he was actual high-weight (127) in a spectacular field that included five horses (Riva Ridge, Secretariat, Cougar II, Kennedy Road, and Key to the Mint) that had been voted year-end champions in North America as a whole or in Canada. So good were their credentials that Onion and Annihilate 'em, both estimable talents, were the rank outsiders. Among them, this bunch had won sixty-three stakes races and earned more than $4.5 million.

The weights assigned by NYRA racing secretary Kenny Noe Jr. were interesting: Riva, at 127, was top-weight, one pound over the scale for older horses at the mile and one-eighth distance at that time of year; Key to the Mint and Cougar II were pegged at scale, 126; Kennedy Road at 121; Annihilate 'em and Onion at 116; and Secretariat at 124, three pounds over scale for three-year-olds, thus a theoretical two pounds over Riva Ridge (at scale weights, 126 on Riva to 121 on Secretariat, there would have been five actual pounds separating them, versus Noe's three-pound spread).

Secretariat went to the track on Wednesday, September 12, for his final pre-Marlboro workout, and this time he gave his Meadow entourage what they were hoping to see.

He was on his toes all the way and bounced back to his stall after burning up the Belmont main track with five furlongs in :57, galloping out an additional furlong in 1:08 4/5, a fifth of a second off the track record.

He had his tone and his attitude back. It was a no-brainer for Turcotte, who could have ridden the rejuvenated Riva Ridge, to opt for Secretariat. By now, he instinctively knew the big colt's movements and moods, and he sensed Secretariat was back in Triple Crown form.

The track was wet in the morning from the previous day's rain but had dried out by mid-afternoon. In the Beldame Stakes, which preceded the Marlboro Cup as part of the CBS telecast, a superb field of fillies and mares that included Convenience, Summer Guest, Light Hearted, and Susan's Girl found themselves looking at the flying heels of the brilliant three-year-old filly Desert Vixen.

Desert Vixen went wire-to-wire and was stronger at the end than at the beginning, winning by eight and a half lengths and equaling the mile and one-eighth track record with a sensational 1:46 1/5 clocking. Clearly, the track was speed favoring.

The atmosphere among the crowd of more than 48,000 was electric as the horses left the paddock for the Marlboro Cup.

Secretariat looked as splendid as ever in the paddock, but he always looked good, and looks had been deceiving in his last start. Could he handle the array of talent facing him, particularly considering the uncertainty surrounding his preparation for the race? Perhaps everyone had been premature in praising this year's three-year-olds; maybe they were average, on the whole, and Secretariat was well above average but not the all-time great that many had proclaimed him after his Triple Crown sweep.

There was sufficient speed in the race to ensure that Secretariat would not lead early, unless he chose to. When the gates opened at 4:50 p.m., Onion went for the lead, with Riva Ridge and Kennedy Road just behind him while Secretariat, breaking from the outside post, got away routinely and stayed well away from the rail as the field zipped through the first quarter in :22 3/5.

Onion had a half-length lead at that point, but these were not claimers behind him, and he was under pressure from the outset, with Riva Ridge, Kennedy Road, and Annihilate 'em in hot pursuit.

They ripped by the half in :45 3/5, in much the same order, although more tightly bunched, and went into the final turn as a foursome, still blazing along.

Looming on their outside, though, was the familiar

blue-and-white blinkered head of the big guy. For Turcotte, it was like old times, the best horse he'd ever seen or been near was firing as he had in the Triple Crown races.

To be sure, there was more to contend with in this race, for these talented veterans had brought their "A" games.

Secretariat stayed wide on the far turn, drifting slightly as he drew a bead on Riva Ridge, who was leading after six furlongs in 1:09 1/5, and Onion. The crowd was on its feet, 48,000 voices in an uproar, watching the race it had hoped for.

Straightened away for home, Secretariat went after his stablemate, collared him at the three-sixteenths pole, and started to pull away in mid-stretch. Riva Ridge wasn't caving in at all; giving his best — and that was championship stuff — he battled hard and willingly, but his year-younger partner was stronger and faster.

Up by two lengths at the eighth pole (the mile in 1:33), Secretariat expanded his lead in the final furlong, finishing with a flourish to win by three and a half lengths over Riva, who had two additional lengths over the fast-finishing Cougar II in third.

There were gasps when attention was directed to the teletimer: Secretariat had beaten the clock again, this time a world-record 1:45 2/5 for nine furlongs! (He was timed, pulling up, in 1:57 4/5 for one and a quarter miles, an unofficial world record.)

The Meadow cup ran over after the Marlboro Cup. Not only had the wonder boy regained his halo, but Riva Ridge had also returned to the top of his class. It was a great day for Laurin and Turcotte, an even better one for the Chenery siblings, who had watched their father's silks finish one-two against one of the best fields ever seen on an American racetrack.

The giant exhalation heard in the aftermath of the race came from CBS and Philip Morris executives, who had gambled on Secretariat's popularity and panache when they created the Marlboro Cup and had gotten the storybook ending they wanted and needed.

Secretariat came out of the race in such good order that it was almost as if he had needed the race to get him back to his best. The Man o' War Stakes at one and a half miles on Belmont's Widener Turf Course loomed as Secretariat's next test. Laurin trained him accordingly for his October 8 grass debut, working him a routine half-mile on the turf in :48 3/5 on September 21, six days after the Marlboro Cup, then a mile in 1:38 over the same surface on September 25.

Riva Ridge was being pointed for the Woodward Stakes at one and a half miles on the dirt on September 29, but Laurin entered both horses with the idea that if the track were dry Riva would run and if it were wet, Secretariat would run. How about having a Triple Crown winner coming off the bench?

This was good in theory, since Riva Ridge could barely stand up on an off track, but it proved problematic in practice.

Rain the night before and the morning of the Woodward left the track sloppy, so Riva stayed dry in his stall while Secretariat went over to the paddock to gird for battle against four others, one of them Cougar II, another the good distance filly Summer Guest, and finally French import Amen II, and a well-bred chestnut four-year-old son of Graustark bred by the fabled King Ranch, now owned by Hobeau Farm, and trained by — guess who? — Allen Jerkens.

Prove Out was the field's longshot at 16.20-1, while Secretariat was 3-10, and Cougar II (2.90-1) was believed to be the red colt's only real threat. The crowd had the latter two handicapped correctly, but they missed Prove Out by a city block.

The Graustark colt took an early lead while rocking along through pedestrian fractions (first quarter in :25, the half in :50), before letting Secretariat slide by him with about five furlongs to run.

Secretariat gained the lead easily enough, going six furlongs in 1:13 2/5 and the mile in 1:37 2/5. But, on the final turn, where he typically opened the throttle and drew away, nothing much happened. Prove Out had taken a breather and was now at Secretariat's flank, then his saddle towel, finally his head.

What was going on here? Prove Out was passing Secretariat, drawing away, gaining a clear and commanding lead. The favorite, while running, simply had no response as Prove Out pulled away to cross the finish line four and a half lengths in front, running twelve sloppy furlongs in a spry 2:25 4/5, which would have been a new American record, save for Secretariat's Belmont epic.

In hindsight, the introductory grass training Secretariat had prior to his unplanned start in the

Woodward on the main track was inadequate for a major race over a mile and a half, especially for a horse that was just getting back to his best form. The Meadow camp had simply been overconfident and should have kept Secretariat on his planned path to the Man o' War, letting him enjoy a relaxed afternoon with Riva Ridge in Barn 5 at Belmont while Prove Out, a high-class talent who would blow away Riva Ridge in the two-mile Jockey Club Gold Cup a month later, did his thing.

With his lesson learned, Laurin sent Secretariat back to the turf, and the results were scintillating.

On the morning of October 5, Secretariat and Turcotte stepped onto the Widener Course for what was intended to be the colt's first "hang 'em on the fence" grass workout. Laurin wanted an indication of how the horse would handle turf footing at race speed.

They were to go five furlongs and gallop out an additional eighth, all at Secretariat's pace. Laurin knew he'd been too casual about the Woodward. His horse hadn't been as fit or as fired up as he needed to be, and the trainer wasn't about to send him into the Man o' War the same way.

Within seconds after Turcotte set him alight that morning, Secretariat displayed his affinity for the surface by singeing a path of his own.

He flew through successive furlongs in :11, :11 2/5, :11 4/5, :10 4/5, and :11 4/5, the quarter in :22 2/5, the half in :45, five-eighths in an awe-inspiring :56 4/5, with the extra furlong tacked on for a final time of 1:09.

Only a few horses would have been capable of achieving such fractions and virtually all of them would have left their next race lying in tatters as a result of so strenuous a workout.

For Secretariat, this was his way of practicing, of getting the physical and mental edge needed to run his next opponents into the ground. Other than in the Whitney, when he was victimized by illness, Secretariat's fastest workouts were followed by his fastest, most explosive victories.

The fifteenth Man o' War Stakes was scheduled for October 8, 1973. It was odd that almost forty years had elapsed after the end of the racing career of America's most famous racehorse before a prominent race was created in his honor. Odder still was that it was run on grass, a surface over which he never competed.

The Man o' War quickly became an important fixture for turf horses, a significant addition to the fall calendar of major grass stakes that helped lure foreign horses, especially European Thoroughbreds, to America to compete with our turf specialists.

Now, Secretariat, the modern horse most often compared to Man o' War, was trying turf for the first time in a race named for the best red colt of another era.

His opposition would include the outstanding four-year-old Tentam, who had become a championship-level grass specialist; the capable and versatile Big Spruce, and another turf star, London Company, who had been considered for the Prix de l'Arc de Triomphe.

Laurin also entered Riva Ridge in the Man o' War, ostensibly in case someone else entered a speed horse as a pacemaker. Riva Ridge had shown no exceptional form on turf, so Laurin's move may have been preemptive.

Regardless, there were no "rabbits" entered, and a seven-horse field made its way onto a firm turf course to contest the Man o' War, one of them being Triangular, a Hobeau Farm-owned, Allen Jerkens-

trained six-year-old with decent form but no pretensions to greatness. His presence at least gave the writers something to speculate about. Could giant killer
Jerkens strike again? Was Secretariat's Woodward
another anomaly, or was he tailing off at the end of a
long season?

Any questions about Secretariat's form, fitness, or
motivation were answered quickly and convincingly
when the gates opened at 4:48 p.m. Secretariat got
away smoothly and found his stride with more alacrity
than usual, much as he had in the Belmont.

He eased between Tentam and longshot Anono as
they moved past the finish line the first time. After
establishing a one and a half-length lead in an opening
quarter of :23 4/5, he lengthened it to three by the
time he had traveled a half-mile in :47.

Secretariat was striding with purpose and power. He
was totally in command of his race, with only Tentam
able to maintain a competitive position. Tentam made
an effort to run at him after the six-furlong marker, but
he made little impression on the Meadow machine.

Secretariat got the six furlongs in 1:11 3/5, and was
still three lengths ahead of Tentam after a mile in 1:36.

The four-year-old, given a breather by jockey Jorge Velasquez, made another run at Secretariat about mid-point of the final turn, but he was chasing one of the best turn runners ever and, again, was unable to dent the chestnut colt's lead.

Secretariat ran his fifth quarter-mile in :24, for a mile and a quarter clocking in 2:00. In the stretch, he was in full flight, driving powerfully, widening his final margin to five lengths over the game Tentam, who was seven and a half lengths ahead of the third horse, Big Spruce.

Secretariat's final time was 2:24 4/5, a new course record by three-fifths of a second and a remarkable race by a horse making his grass debut. Perhaps Kent Hollingsworth had been right; maybe Secretariat should have taken up the Arc challenge.

It was too late for that now, and Tweedy and Laurin were down to one final decision: end it after the Man o' War and send him to Claiborne Farm for the next chapter; run him one more time in the two-mile Jockey Club Gold Cup on dirt or the mile-and-a-half Washington, D.C., International at Laurel on turf, America's oldest major grass race; or travel to Canada for Woodbine's Canadian International Championship at one and five-eighth miles on the turf.

Canada it would be, a salute to Laurin's and Turcotte's Canadian heritage, and a chance to show-case Secretariat to an international audience. A week after the Man o' War, Laurin gave the colt a mainte-nance workout on Belmont's turf, where he sped six furlongs in 1:11 2/5, cruising.

Shipped north to Woodbine, where he was likely to encounter deeper, softer turf than he had experienced, Secretariat made believers out of Canadian clockers with a five-furlong blowout in :57 3/5 the week of the Canadian International. This work was accomplished "around the dogs," the orange cones set up about thir-ty feet off the inner rail to protect the inside part of the course.

Although Tentam's owner, E.P. Taylor, was easily the most important figure on the Canadian racing scene, he re-routed his horse to the D.C. International, preferring to skip another confrontation with the three-year-old superstar.

Even without Tentam, Woodbine managed to hus-tle eleven horses to face Secretariat including Canada's best: Kennedy Road, Big Spruce, Golden Don, Presidial (owned by Taylor's Windfields Farm), Triangular, and Twice Lucky.

Sadly for Turcotte, a riding infraction that occurred earlier in the fall would force him to miss the race. New York-based jockey Eddie Maple, who had subbed for him on Riva Ridge in the Marlboro Cup, picked up the mount on Secretariat in the Canadian International, with the suspended Turcotte watching as a television commentator.

Maple's job was to keep his horse out of trouble and let him run his race. He was the pilot; Secretariat, the aircraft.

Race day was cold and drizzly, an unpleasant afternoon to be outdoors. The turf course was listed as firm but had more give than Secretariat was used to, making the mile and five-eighths a good test of stamina.

The race belonged to two horses, Kennedy Road, who had ownership only through Secretariat's sufferance for the first mile, and the champ, who swallowed up Kennedy Road when asked to do so and left the rest for dead.

That pair had brief contact when Kennedy Road, tiring, bumped Secretariat slightly as he went by him nearing the final turn. Secretariat wanted to bump back, but Maple gathered the colt and reminded him of the business ahead.

Running relentlessly, in complete control of the race, Secretariat opened a twelve-length lead in early stretch and still held sway by six and a half lengths at the finish, the time in 2:41 4/5.

Coming through the fog and mist of afternoon twilight, breathing vapor as he flew home, Secretariat looked like a medieval warhorse carrying his master home to castle and fair damsel.

The grand parade had ended.

Secretariat finished 1973 with nine wins in twelve starts, a single season record of $860,404 in earnings, and a two-year record of sixteen wins in twenty-one starts, with $1,316,808 in earnings. He was again named Horse of the Year, as well as champion three-year-old male and champion grass horse.

Statistics and titles could not begin to measure the enormous impact his sixteen months of racing did for a sport seeking a hero, trying to recapture its stature. Not only was he "the complete package," but he also redefined that aphorism.

Veteran horsemen admired his conformation, clean limbs, and overwhelming power. Turf historians were hard pressed to find a horse that created such expectations, then exceeded them. He drew enormous media attention and created thousands of new racing fans, many of them young people drawn to his good looks and the dominance of his best performances.

He left us with a mosaic of racing memories, best recalled in the most dazzling two and a half minutes in the history of racing, his own Belmont masterpiece. He lifted us, made us feel better about our sport and ourselves, let us brush with perfection.

Rating schemes of any sort are matters of considerable debate, and few racing aficionados attempted to compare Secretariat statistically to other great horses, but comparisons are part of the fun of any sport, so upon his retirement it was common to see articles offering opinions as to the relative merits of Secretariat versus Citation, Man o' War, Count Fleet, Native Dancer, Tom Fool, Buckpasser, Dr. Fager, Kelso, et al.

The consensus, and there really wasn't one, had him grouped with Man o' War and Citation, with an occasional Native Dancer or Count Fleet tossed into the mix.

Charlie Hatton was not at all unsure of what he'd seen, nor inclined to waste time on comparisons. In his year-end review of 1973 in the *American Racing Manual* he wrote:

"Secretariat was a Superhorse, rather than a transient Horse of the Year. Veteran turfmen, sophisticates of deep experience and broad, informed tastes, pronounced him 'The Horse of the Century.' He is the only Thoroughbred ever given this identity on an official program.

"Secretariat appealed to all levels of the sporting society, professional and public alike. His distinction is based on the awareness and judgment of the former rather than the idolatry of the latter.

"Exterminator and Man o' War have come and gone since the present writer's first acquaintance with the sport. Impressions of long standing tend to become fixed and assume a prescriptive right not to be questioned. But Secretariat is the most capable horse we ever saw, and geriatrics defeat any thought of seeing his like again."

Kent Hollingsworth's predecessor at *The Blood-Horse*, the scholarly and gifted Joe Estes, had once written an ode to Man o' War, a portion of which said:

A foal is born at midnight
And in the frosty morn
The horseman eyes him fondly,
And a secret hope is born
But breathe in not, nor whisper
For fear of a neighbor's scorn.
He's a chestnut colt, and he's
got a star.
He may be another Man o' War.
Nay, say it aloud—be shameless.
Dream and hope and yearn,
For there's never a man among you
But waits for his return.

For Charlie Hatton, the second coming of Man o'
War was a *fait accompli*. Hatton would meet his Maker
on March 14, 1975, confident that he had been privi-
leged to live long enough to see the new and — in his
view — improved Man o' War.

CHAPTER 10

A Big Heart

A once in a lifetime two-year run had ended for Penny Tweedy, Lucien Laurin, Ron Turcotte, Eddie Sweat, Charlie Davis, and those working in Laurin's barn or back home in Virginia at The Meadow.

Now, it was Seth Hancock's turn to shape the next phase of Secretariat's career. The youthful Hancock had assembled a blue-chip syndicate in the winter of 1973, nursed them through the Wood Memorial aftershock and celebrated the Triple Crown experience.

Although Secretariat represented Hancock's first major stallion deal as the pilot of the Claiborne ship, he well understood the challenges inherent in making the red horse the successful sire people expected him to become. Thus, putting together a syndicate with many of the sport's leading private and commercial breeders had been an essential first step.

Trying to figure out how to match mares to Secretariat, from both a pedigree and conformation standpoint, was next. Clearly, people who had paid $190,000 a share for the right to breed to Secretariat (and had, in some instances, been offered $500,000 to part with their share) were going to send him mares of quality, stakes winners and/or producers from female families with exceptional production records.

The guessing game began with trying to analyze just what type of mare might mate best with the big colt. His pedigree, while of the highest order, provided little help in gauging his type. He was certainly not a typical Bold Ruler, despite his early display of class as a two-year-old. In hindsight, it is clear that he was a throwback to the old concept of a classic horse: a true stayer with exceptional speed. In other words, he probably would have done best with speed-oriented mares.

As for pedigree, he was the son of one of history's most successful stallions, out of a mare who had previously produced a top-class international sire in Sir Gaylord. Bold Ruler as a sire of sires was not a finished book when Secretariat came along. The aging stallion had many sons at stud and a number of them had begun their stud careers promisingly.

In fact, after Secretariat, Bold Ruler-line racehorses dominated the rest of the seventies. His sons or grandsons would sire six horses that would win ten of the eighteen American Triple Crown races from 1974 through 1979, including Triple Crown winner Seattle Slew and the brilliant Spectacular Bid.

The gentlemanly sports editor and columnist for the *Dayton Daily News*, Sy Burick, perhaps offered the best and most succinct view of Secretariat's new life when he wrote about how much he envied the horse: "He's young, he's rich, he's good looking, has all of his hair, and his entire sex life is in front of him."

No horse had ever gone to the breeding shed — except, possibly, Man o' War — with such a towering reputation as a racehorse and specimen of the breed.

Secretariat, standing at one of America's most prestigious breeding farms, his shares in the hands of breeders owning numerous superior broodmares, would have a better chance to be a good sire than the horse to whom he was most often compared.

Success at stud can be measured in many ways, but ultimately, a stallion's stud career is judged by his aggregate number of stakes winners and, in particular, his percentage of winners to foals and winners to starters.

Since such records have been maintained, the very best sires, such as Bold Ruler, Nasrullah, and Northern Dancer, got 23 percent stakes winners from foals. A world-class sire will average somewhere in the mid to high teens, and anything below 10 percent is regarded as unexceptional.

Secretariat didn't figure to be Bold Ruler, at least statistically, but most observers believed he would get horses that would be formidable around two turns, could run on dirt or grass, and would get better with age. He might get precocious two-year-olds, but he would be forgiven that lapse if his offspring could perform when the money and prestige were on the line at age three and beyond.

Once his first crop, foals of 1975, reached the races, it soon became evident that Secretariat was unlikely to be an exceptional stallion. They were a mixed bag physically and didn't get to the races quickly or show much early ability, although they came from high-class race mares or producers.

There were only two stakes winners in that first crop, neither of them anything special. The Thoroughbred marketplace is a coldly efficient place, and the buzz on Secretariat was not good by the time his next crop arrived at the races. That group was better, highlighted by the classy multiple stakes winner General Assembly, who won the Travers Stakes in record time, and the speedy filly Terlingua, a brilliant and versatile sort who would later become the dam of the great sire Storm Cat.

The next crop featured five moderate stakes winners, and by the end of the seventies, the evidence was strong that Secretariat would be far better remembered as a runner than as a stallion. He was not a complete failure, and there was always a chance that he would get a top-class horse here and there, but his percentages of winners and stakes winners were moderate, particularly considering the quality of his mates, and he was not siring major race winners with any consistency.

When the occasional good ones came along, they could be very good indeed, such as the magnificent Lady's Secret, who showed hints of a decent future at two with victories in 1984 in the Moccasin and Wavy Waves stakes at Hollywood Park.

At three she was sensational, winning ten of her seventeen starts, all stakes victories, including the Beldame, Ruffian, Test, Maskette, and Ballerina stakes. She earned $994,349 that year and was the best three-year-old filly in America in the fall.

At four the daughter of the Icecapade mare Great Lady M. was even better, winning ten of fifteen starts. She beat boys in the grade I Whitney Handicap at Saratoga, a race her sire lost, and won seven other grade I races, among them the Breeders' Cup Distaff, Santa Margarita Invitational, and the Shuvee Handicap.

She was brilliant on both coasts, earned $1,871,053, was named champion older mare and — rarity of rarities for a female — Horse of the Year. Her final career tally: twenty-five wins in forty-five starts (twenty-two stakes wins) and $3,021,325 in earnings.

By the mid-1980s no one was expecting Secretariat to duplicate himself, and he would not, but his 1985 foal class would contain his closest approximation, and a reasonable facsimile, if not for long.

His name was Risen Star, and he was a massive colt, bigger and more substantial than even his sire. Out of the His Majesty mare Ribbon, he was bred to run all day but showed enough speed at two to win a small stakes race at Louisiana Downs.

At three the powerhouse dark bay youngster was second in the Lecomte Handicap at the Fair Grounds, then went on a tear, winning the Louisiana Derby Trial Stakes, the Louisiana Derby itself, and the Lexington Stakes at Keeneland. Well liked in the Kentucky Derby, he was third, after a troubled trip, behind the winner, the filly Winning Colors.

Trained by his irrepressible owner, Louie Roussel, Risen Star beat Winning Colors and Forty Niner in the Preakness, then stunned the racing world with a fourteen and three-quarters length win in the Belmont, running one and a half miles in 2:26 2/5, the third fastest Belmont to date.

A persistent tendon problem stopped his career at that point, but he had, for a few short weeks, reawakened the echoes. At the end of the 1988 season, he was voted champion three-year-old male over Forty Niner and Seeking the Gold, retiring with eight wins in eleven starts and $2,029,845.

In September 1989, Secretariat was diagnosed with laminitis, the incurable foot disease that often causes extensive suffering in the afflicted horse. Although Claiborne's vets battled the disease, they knew they were fighting a rear-guard action.

Secretariat, as gorgeous and game as ever, fought the infection for a month, but finally the pain was too much and he was euthanized on Wednesday, October 4, at 11:45 a.m.

It was as if the racing world came to a momentary halt, tearfully recalling its lost hero, reliving those marvelous moments in 1972 and '73 when this larger-than-life colt, built to perfection and granted unparalleled gifts, had drawn America's attention to the racetrack.

Television and print media treated his death as they would have that of a human celebrity, and thousands of people remembered the day they first became racing enthusiasts because of his meteoric and majestic performances. Hundreds waited outside the Claiborne gates to pay their respects to an equine hero who was an American icon.

The king was dead. His legend would be ever-present.

As good luck would have it, there was one final good one in the pipeline, a colt named Tinners Way, foaled in 1990, out of Devon Diva, by The Minstrel.

After beginning his career in England, where he won two stakes, he was brought home at age four and became one of the country's leading handicap performers, winning two runnings of the Pacific Classic at Del Mar, and the Californian Stakes at Hollywood Park. He also equaled Del Mar's one and a quarter mile track record with a 1:59 2/5 clocking, and Hollywood's one and one-eighth mile mark with a 1:46 3/5 tally.

Tinners Way earned $1,846,546 in a distinguished career, and left his sire's legion of followers with a few final positive memories.

In aggregate, Secretariat was neither a bad sire nor an outstanding one. He was solidly in the middle, capable of getting an occasional star-quality horse, such as Lady's Secret and Risen Star but unable to deliver the high-level consistency widely expected of him. His fifty-six stakes winners (8 percent of his foals) were decent enough for the average stallion, but Secretariat was not supposed to be average.

As it became clear that he was not going to match his sire's or grandsire's stud exploits, the quality of his mates declined, although it was never bad, for with Secretariat, breeders always held onto a glimmer of hope, the idea that their mare just might be the one with the right gene pool to produce lightning one more time.

His commercial record was good, with 259 of his yearlings selling for an average of just over $200,000 a piece.

At the end of 2001, thirty-eight of his sons were at stud worldwide, although none have distinguished themselves, and it seems unlikely his male line will be meaningful in the future. As a broodmare sire, however, he has been something special. His daughters have always been highly prized, and they have become more so after many of them produced good stakes horses (151 stakes winners by the end of 2001).

The list of top-class horses out of Secretariat mares is almost endless. The millionaires among them include A.P. Indy, Dare and Go, Al Mamoon, Chief's Crown, Fruits of Love, Atticus, Istabraq, and Summer Squall.

Secretariat is also the broodmare sire of many leading sires, including Storm Cat, A.P. Indy, Gone West, and Summer Squall.

That Secretariat was a disappointment as a sire, and he was, reflected the level of expectation surrounding him when he arrived at Claiborne. Triple Crown winners before him had ranged from outright stud failures

(Sir Barton and Omaha), to below average (Citation and Whirlaway), to moderately good (Gallant Fox), to exceptional (Count Fleet and War Admiral), to sterile (Assault, who never sired a foal).

But, Secretariat was supposed to be different. People wanted him to succeed as a sire because, well, that's the way fairy tales are supposed to end.

The astute, always to the point British bloodstock writer Tony Morris captured Secretariat's life after racing in a profound and succinct way in his book, *Thoroughbred Stallions*:

"There are all manner of reasons why good — even great racehorses fail to excel at stud, but it is not always easy to identify them. It would seem ridiculous to suggest that he lacked opportunity, yet it is possible that the mares he had were not those most suitable for him. Because he was precocious and had tremendous speed, he was perceived by many breeders as basically a speed horse, in the Bold Ruler mould. That is one thing he never was...in crude terms he was basically a stayer, a resolute galloper, and a machine at that. His action was more that of a greyhound than of a racehorse. How do you mate a creature so different from the rest of this race? Perhaps we should have suspected that he would get only the odd good one, thrown up by chance rather than by design.

"Secretariat did represent a breakthrough. In physique and performance he set new standards in the development of the Thoroughbred, but it was not within his powers to take it a stage further. For all he seemed on that glorious day at Belmont in June 1973, he was only mortal."

Or was he?

A necropsy performed by Dr. Thomas Swerczek, professor of veterinary science at the University of Kentucky, immediately after Secretariat's death revealed that the red horse's heart was almost twice as big as the heart of an average horse. It was not abnormal in any other way, just bigger.

In a sense, this discovery validated Morris' view of Secretariat. He was physical perfection, and then some, a once in a lifetime gift of nature.

Such gifts are seldom seen, never replicated.

SECRETARIAT

EPILOGUE

Big Red vs. Big Red

W hich Big Red was the Bigger Red?

We, of course, will never know, which is probably better, because horse racing thrives on its mythology and tradition, perhaps more than any other sport.

The careers of Man o' War and Secretariat, completed fifty-three years apart, were amazingly similar; likewise was their stature in American folklore.

Separately, and collectively, they wrote epics that have made their legends larger through succeeding generations.

Secretariat elicited human responses as had no Thoroughbred since Man o' War. He was headline news, in his great and not-so-great moments. He was telegenic in the age of television, which magnified both his greatness and his failures. By the end of his racing career, he was the most photographed, written about, talked about horse in Thoroughbred racing history, an American idol.

The same could be said of the horse to whom he was and is most compared: Man o' War. A copper-coated chestnut of ample proportions, similar to Secretariat, Man o' War exuded energy and power, with a stride measuring twenty-five to twenty-seven feet and a physique that made him a man among boys.

He was so consistently spectacular, so dominating, that his exploits were front-page sports news. Man o' War's fame, though, did not stop with newspaper headlines. So theatrical were his performances that he soon achieved a reputation reaching well beyond the racing universe.

He was a true sports legend in the early 1920s, a name as well known as those of the human superstars of his era, figures such as baseball greats Ty Cobb and Babe Ruth, football legend Red Grange, or boxing champions Jack Dempsey and Gene Tunney.

Physically, the two horses were similar in stature and girth, correctly made, with great shoulders, deep chests, powerful hindquarters, and strong, well-made legs. Secretariat was the flashier, thanks to the generous splashes of white on three of his legs and his face.

He was also slightly larger than Man o' War.

Suffice it to say that both horses stood out from their respective crowds.

Both were well-bred. Man o' War was by the leading sire of his day, Fair Play, out of a multiple stakes producer, Mahubah, herself by English Triple Crown winner Rock Sand. Both came from highly successful breeding operations, Man o' War being bred by August Belmont II, the most important racing man of his era.

Each was bred to be a classic horse, and so they both became, but they also were high-class two-year-olds, something not necessarily compatible with either of their pedigrees or physical make-ups.

As two-year-olds both demonstrated exceptional ability from the onset of their racing careers, and it is interesting to contrast them from that point onward.

Man o' War at two:

• Showed unusual precocity well before his first race, earlier than Secretariat, who didn't seem to get with it right away.

• Was usually on or near the lead in his races, although there is no indication that he was a hard puller or die-hard speed horse.

• Won nine of ten starts, six of them carrying 130 pounds, an unheard of impost for a two-year-old today, not as uncommon in his era. What was uncommon was his ability to concede lots of weight and still dominate his competition.

• Was already considered a champion in the making by the time of the Saratoga race meet, during which he was beaten for the only time, losing to Upset while carrying fifteen more pounds and plagued by both a slow start and a miserable ride by his jockey, Johnny Loftus.

• Was not asked to race past six furlongs, in keeping with the custom of the day.

• Was assigned 136 pounds by a *Daily Racing Form* handicapper giving a mythical rating to the season's best two-year-olds. The next horse in the rating received 120 pounds, such was the dominance of Man o' War in everyone's thinking.

Secretariat at two:

• A bit slow to figure things out, but ready to be a star by the time his career got underway in July, a month after Man o' War had debuted fifty-three years earlier.

• Already had a great reputation when he arrived at Saratoga, where he only enhanced it.

• Lost twice, one on a disqualification, but was clearly the best horse in both of his losses.

• Never carried more than 122 pounds, but faced larger, probably more competitive fields than did Man o' War.

• Established a come-from-behind style that was of his own choosing, but had strong acceleration and the ability to sustain it.

Based on their two-year-old records, there is little to differentiate the two horses. Man o' War came to hand more readily and demonstrated a higher degree of brilliance, but Secretariat, while slower to find his best stride, was also head and shoulders above his contemporaries by year end.

Man o' War at three:

• Was eleven for eleven, his closest winning margin being one and a half lengths.

• Carried 138 and 135 pounds to easy victories.

• Set seven track records while equaling another and set five American records (a mile in 1:35 4/5; a mile and one-eighth in 1:49 1/5; a mile and three-eighths in 2:14 1/5; a mile and a half in 2:28 4/5; and a mile and five-eighths in 2:40 4/5). The longer distance records stood for many years, a tribute to Man o' War's massive talent in an era when racetrack surfaces were typically deeper and more inconsistent than today.

Secretariat at three:

• Was nine for twelve at three, including one loss when he was almost certainly affected by a virus; his other two defeats, while not disgraceful, were less explainable.

• Set or equaled five, probably six track records, counting his disputed Preakness, and established two world records. His times were uniformly faster than Man o' War's for comparable distances, but he was racing over more finely honed surfaces.

• Was as effective on turf as on dirt, something Man o' War never had a chance to demonstrate.

• Never carried more than 126 pounds, although he won six out of seven times with that weight, but likely faced more uniformly high-caliber competition.

Both horses retired after their three-year-old seasons, having accomplished about all that could reasonably be expected of them. Man o' War's overall record — twenty wins in twenty-one starts — was nominally

superior to Secretariat's sixteen wins in the same number of starts, but Secretariat faced more good horses, if
not better ones.

They were both outstanding stayers with powerful,
relentless strides and high cruising rates. Man o' War
might have had more natural speed, or at least the ability to find high gear faster, but Secretariat, once in full
flight, seemed to be a bottomless well.

Each horse, at his best, thoroughly dominated his
opposition, although Secretariat's Belmont was incom-
parable, even by Man o' War's standards.

The two were the complete package of size, looks,
speed, stamina, durability, competitiveness, and charisma. They captured the public's imagination and ran so
far so fast that they came to be regarded as statistical
anomalies, unique presences far superior to their contemporaries and those beyond.

If Man o' War set the standard for American
Thoroughbreds in the twentieth century, Secretariat
met that standard and might have elevated it.

In a head-to-head meeting, Man o' War's natural
early speed would have given him a tactical advantage,
but Secretariat proved able to cope with a variety of

tactical circumstances, running faster as the race progressed.

The romantic ideal is that the two would have come to the finish line together, two mighty gladiators straining to win the race of a lifetime. Practically, a review of their records and racing tendencies, as remotely anecdotal as such a comparison might be, suggests that the ideal is probably reasonable.

In the stretch run of racing history, they're racing side by side, swapping the lead with each bob of their respective heads.

It's Secretariat, now Man o' War, now Secretariat, now Man o' War, and as they hit the wire in this race of races, the winner is the chestnut son of...

Wow, what a finish! Those two looked like they could have gone around again lapped on each other.

Best race I ever saw!

They'll be talking about this one for years to come.

SECRETARIAT's PEDIGREE

		Nearco, 1935	Pharos Nogara
	Nasrullah, 1940		
		Mumtaz Begum, 1932	Blenheim II Mumtaz Maha
BOLD RULER, dk b, 1954		Discovery, 1931	Display Ariadne
	Miss Disco, 1944		
		Outdone, 1936	Pompey Sweep Out
SECRETARIAT, chestnut colt, 1970		Prince Rose, 1928	Rose Prince Indolence
	Princequillo, 1940		
		Cosquilla, 1933	Papyrus Quick Though
SOMETHINGROYAL, b, 1952		Caruso, 1927	Polymelian Sweet Music
	Imperatrice, 1938		
		Cinquepace, 1934	Brown Bud Assignation

SECRETARIAT's RACE RECORD

Secretariat

ch. c. 1970, by Bold Ruler (Nasrullah)–Somethingroyal, by Princequillo — **Lifetime record: 21 16 3 1 $1,316,808**

Own.– Meadow Stable
Br.– Meadow Stud Inc (Va)
Tr.– L. Laurin

28Oct73- 8WO	fm 1⅝Ⓣ	:47^2 1:37^3 2:41^4	3↑	Can Int'l-G2	12	2	2$^{1\frac12}$	1^5	1^{12}	1$^{6\frac12}$	Maple E	117	b	*.20	96-04	Secretariat117$^{6\frac12}$BigSpruce126$^{1\frac12}$GoldenDon117$^{\frac34}$	Ridden out	12
8Oct73- 7Bel	fm 1½Ⓣ	:47 1:11^3 2:00 2:24^4	3↑	Man o' War-G1	3	1	1^3	1$^{1\frac12}$	1^3	1^5	Turcotte R	121	b	*.50	103-01	Secretariat121^{5}Tentam126$^{7\frac12}$Big Spruce126$^{\frac12}$	Ridden out	7
29Sep73- 7Bel	sly 1½	:50 1:13^2 2:01^4 2:25^4	3↑	Woodward-G1	5	2	2$^{\frac12}$	1^{hd}	2$^{1\frac12}$	2$^{4\frac12}$	Turcotte R	119	b	*.30	86-15	ProveOut126$^{4\frac12}$Secretariat119^{11}CougarII126$^{\frac12}$	Best of rest	5
15Sep73- 7Bel	fst 1⅛	:45^3 1:09^1 1:33 1:45^2	3↑	Marl Cup Inv'l H 250k	7	5	5$^{1\frac14}$	3$^{\frac12}$	1^2	1$^{3\frac12}$	Turcotte R	124	b	*.40e	104-07	Secretariat124$^{3\frac12}$Riva Ridge127^{2}Cougar II126$^{6\frac12}$	Ridden out	7
4Aug73- 7Sar	fst 1⅛	:47^4 1:11 1:36 1:49^1	3↑	Whitney H-G2	3	4	3^1	2$^{\frac12}$	2^{hd}	2^1	Turcotte R	119	b	*.10	94-15	Onion119^{1}Secretariat119$^{\frac12}$Rule by Reason119^2	Weakened	5
30Jun73- 8AP	fst 1⅛	:48 1:11^1 1:35 1:47		Invitational 125k	4	1	1^3	1$^{2\frac12}$	1^6	1^9	Turcotte R	126	b	*.05	99-17	Secretariat126^{9}My Gallant120^{nk}Our Native120^{17}	Easily	4
9Jun73- 8Bel	fst 1½	:46^1 1:09^4 1:59 2:24		Belmont-G1	1	1	1^{hd}	1^{20}	1^{28}	1^{31}	Turcotte R	126	b	*.10	113-05	Secretariat126^{31}TwiceaPrince126$^{\frac12}$MyGllnt126^{13}	Ridden out	5
19May73- 8Pim	fst 1$\frac{3}{16}$	:48^1 1:11^2 1:35^3 1:54^2		Preakness-G1	3	4	1$^{\frac12}$	1$^{2\frac12}$	1$^{2\frac12}$	1$^{2\frac12}$	Turcotte R	126	b	*.30	98-13	Secretariat126$^{2\frac12}$Sham126^{8}Our Native126^1	Handily	6
	Daily Racing Form time 1:53 2/5																	
5May73- 9CD	fst 1¼	:47^2 1:11^4 1:36^1 1:59^2		Ky Derby-G1	10	11	6$^{9\frac12}$	2$^{\frac12}$	1$^{\frac12}$	1$^{2\frac12}$	Turcotte R	126	b	*1.50e	103-10	Secretariat126$^{2\frac12}$Sham126^{8}Our Native126$^{\frac12}$	Handily	13
21Apr73- 7Aqu	fst 1⅛	:48^1 1:12^1 1:36^4 1:49^4		Wood Memorial-G1	6	7	6^6	5$^{5\frac12}$	4$^{5\frac12}$	3^4	Turcotte R	126	b	*.30e	83-17	Angle Light126^{hd}Sham126^{4}Secretariat126$^{\frac12}$	Wide,hung	8
7Apr73- 7Aqu	fst 1	:23^1 :45^1 1:08^3 1:33^2		Gotham-G2	3	3	1^{hd}	1^2	1$^{\frac12}$	1^3	Turcotte R	126	b	*.10	100-08	Secretariat126^{3}ChampagneCharl117^{10}Flush117$^{2\frac12}$	Ridden out	6
17Mar73- 7Aqu	sly 7f	:22^1 :44^4 1:10 1:23^1		Bay Shore-G3	4	5	5^6	5^3	1^{hd}	1$^{4\frac12}$	Turcotte R	126	b	*.20	85-17	Secretarit126$^{4\frac12}$ChmpgnChrl118$^{2\frac12}$Impcunous126^{no}	Mild drive	6
18Nov72- 8GS	fst 1$\frac{1}{16}$	:24^1 :47^2 1:12 1:44^2		Garden State 298k	6	6	4$^{6\frac14}$	3^3	1$^{1\frac12}$	1$^{3\frac12}$	Turcotte R	122	b	*.10e	83-23	Secretariat122$^{3\frac12}$Angle Light122$^{\frac12}$Step Nicely122$^{\frac34}$	Handily	6
28Oct72- 7Lrl	sly 1$\frac{1}{16}$	:22^4 :45^4 1:11^2 1:42^4		Lrl Futurity 133k	5	6	5^{10}	5^3	1^5	1^8	Turcotte R	122	b	*.10e	99-14	Secretariat122^{8}Stop the Music122^{8}Angle Light122^1	Easily	6
14Oct72- 7Bel	fst 1	:22^4 :45^1 1:09^4 1:35		Champagne 146k	4	11	9$^{8\frac12}$	5$^{3\frac12}$	1$^{\frac12}$	1^2	Turcotte R	122	b	*.70e	97-12	[D]Secretariat122^{2}StoptheMusic122^{2}StepNicly122$^{1\frac12}$	Bore in	12
	Disqualified and placed second																	
16Sep72- 7Bel	fst 6½f	:22^3 :45^3 1:10 1:16^2		Futurity 144k	4	5	6$^{5\frac12}$	5$^{3\frac12}$	1^2	1$^{1\frac34}$	Turcotte R	122	b	*.20	98-09	Secretariat122$^{1\frac34}$StoptheMusic122^{5}SwiftCourr122$^{2\frac12}$	Handily	7
26Aug72- 7Sar	fst 6½f	:22^4 :46^3 1:09^4 1:16^1		Hopeful 86k	8	8	9$^{6\frac12}$	1^{hd}	1^4	1^5	Turcotte R	121	b	*.30	97-12	Secretariat121^{5}FlighttoGlory121^{nk}StopthMusc121^2	Handily	9
16Aug72- 7Sar	fst 6f	:22^4 :46^1 1:10		Sanford 27k	2	5	5^4	4^1	1$^{\frac12}$	1^3	Turcotte R	121	b	1.50	96-14	Secretariat121^{3}Lnd'sChf121^{6}NorthstrDncr121$^{3\frac12}$	Ridden out	5
31Jly72- 4Sar	fst 6f	:23^1 :46^2 1:10^4		Alw 9000	4	7	7$^{3\frac34}$	3$^{\frac12}$	1^{hd}	1$^{1\frac12}$	Turcotte R	118	b	*.40	92-13	Secretariat118$^{1\frac12}$Russ Miron118^{7}Joe Iz118$^{2\frac12}$	Ridden out	7
15Jly72- 4Aqu	fst 6f	:22^1 :45^2 1:10^3		©Md Sp Wt	8	11	6$^{6\frac12}$	4^3	1$^{\frac12}$	1^6	Feliciano P^5	113	b	*1.30	90-14	Secretariat113^{6}Master Achiever118$^{\frac34}$Be on It118^4	Handily	11
4Jly72- 2Aqu	fst 5½f	:22^2 :46^1 :58^4 1:05		©Md Sp Wt	2	11	10^7	10$^{8\frac34}$	7$^{5\frac12}$	4$^{1\frac14}$	Feliciano P^5	113	b	*3.10	87-11	Herbull118^{nk}Master Achiever118^{1}Fleet 'n Royal118^{no}		12
	Impeded,rallied																	

Copyrighted © 2000 by Daily Racing Form, Inc. Reprinted from the book "Champions" (DRF Press)

Index

217

Photo Credits

Cover photo: (Bob Coglianese)

Page 1: Secretariat returning from Preakness (Tony Leonard); Secretariat head shot (Anne M. Eberhardt)

Page 2: Nasrullah (The Blood-Horse); Bold Ruler (The Blood-Horse); Princequillo (The Blood-Horse); Somethingroyal (Allen Studio)

Page 3: Penny Tweedy with Secretariat and Eddie Sweat (The Blood-Horse); Mr. and Mrs. Christopher Chenery (Paul Schafer); Meadow Stud (Susan Thomas)

Page 4: Secretariat with Eddie Sweat (Tony Leonard); with Lucien Laurin (The Blood-Horse); Ron Turcotte (The Blood-Horse); Turcotte, Laurin, and Tweedy (John C. Wyatt); Eddie Maple (Barbara D. Livingston)

Page 5: Secretariat at Saratoga (Susan Thomas); Secretariat winning the Sanford (UPI); Winning the Futurity (Bob Coglianese)

Page 6: Winning the Champagne (Bob Coglianese); Winning the Laurel Futurity (Jerry Frutkoff and Jim McCue); Winning the Garden State (Jim Raftery)

Page 7: Winning the Bay Shore (Bob Coglianese); Winning the Gotham (Bob Coglianese); Gotham winner's circle (Bob Coglianese)

Page 8-9: Derby post parade (The Blood-Horse); Winning the Derby (The Blood-Horse); Derby winner's circle (The Blood-Horse); With Derby trophy (The Blood-Horse); Secretariat going back to barn (The Blood-Horse)

Page 10-11: Winning the Preakness (The Blood-Horse); Preakness winner's circle (S. Siciliano); In the Belmont paddock (The Blood-Horse); The Belmont stretch run (Ray Woolfe Jr.); After the Belmont (Ray Woolfe Jr.)

Page 12: Secretariat and Riva Ridge (The Blood-Horse); Secretariat and Penny Tweedy (Paul Schafer); Secretariat at Belmont barn (The Blood-Horse); Secretariat grazing near sign (Paul Schafer)

Page 13: The Whitney upset (Bob Coglianese); Winning the Marlboro Cup (NYRA); After the Marlboro Cup (Bob Coglianese)

Page 14: Working on turf (Bob Coglianese); Winning the Man o' War (The Blood-Horse); Winning the Canadian International (Michael Burns)

Page 15: Lady's Secret (Four Footed Fotos); General Assembly (Barbara D. Livingston); Risen Star (Bob Coglianese); Weekend Surprise (Anne M. Eberhardt); Terlingua (Anne M. Eberhardt)

Page 16: Secretariat conformation (Anne M. Eberhardt); Gravestone (Shigeki Kikkawa); Statue (Barbara D. Livingston)

ABOUT THE

AUTHOR

T imothy T. Capps has been involved in nearly every aspect of the Thoroughbred industry. During the 1970s and mid-80s Capps served as editor of *The Thoroughbred Record*, a leading industry monthly. In the mid-80s he ventured into the high-stakes stallion market as an executive with Matchmaker, a company that sold stallion seasons and shares.

From there he went to work at the Maryland Jockey Club, which oversees racing at Pimlico and Laurel Park. After serving as vice president of the Maryland Horse Breeders Association and editor and publisher of *MidAtlantic Thoroughbred*, Capps returned in 2001 to the Maryland Jockey Club as executive vice president.

Capps is the author of previous Thoroughbred Legends titles *Spectacular Bid* and *Affirmed and Alydar*. He resides in Columbia, Maryland.